John H. Morgan

GERIATRIC PSYCHOTHERAPY

Essays in Clinical Practice and Counseling Psychology

John H. Morgan

GERIATRIC PSYCHOTHERAPY
Essays in Clinical Practice and Counseling Psychology

John H. Morgan

978-155605-507-2 Paperback
978-155605-508-9 E Book

Published by Wyndham Hall Press

John H. Morgan

INTRODUCTION 9

CHAPTER ONE

Palliative Psychotherapeutic Options in Geriatric Depression
Management: Evidence-Based Non-Pharmacological Treatments
in Review 11

CHAPTER TWO

The Interpersonal Psychotherapy of Harry Stack Sullivan:
Remembering the Legacy 32

CHAPTER THREE

What to Do When there is Nothing to Do:

The Psychotherapeutic Value of Meaning Therapy in the
Treatment of Late Life Depression 49

CHAPTER FOUR

Late-Life Depression and the Counseling Agenda:

Exploring Geriatric Logotherapy as a Treatment Modality..........65

CHAPTER FIVE

Geriatric Logotherapy: Exploring the Psychotherapeutics of
Memory in Treating the Elderly

CHAPTER SIX

Medication and Counseling in Psychiatric Practice: Biogenic
Psycho-pharmacology and Psychogenic Psychotherapy

(Partnering in the Treatment of Mental Illness)............................93

CHAPTER SEVEN

A Tribute to Carl Rogers' Celebrated Classic *On Becoming a Person (1961)* 96

CHAPTER EIGHT

Psychology of Religion and the Books that Made it Happen 116

CHAPTER NINE

Personal Meaning as Therapy: The Interpretive Hermeneutic of Viktor Frankl 152

CHAPTER TEN

Cognitive Behavioral Therapy and Reminiscence Therapy in the Treatment of Depression:

A Convergent Palliative Care Methodology in Geriatric Psychotherapy...167

CHAPTER ELEVEN

Retirement and Mental Health: A Decade of Research in Review 192

CHAPTER TWELVE

Geriatric Narcissism: The Psychotherapeutics of Self-Regard among the Elderly...215

ABOUT THE AUTHOR 242

-

ACKNOWLEDGMENTS

"Palliative Psychotherapy in the Treatment of Geriatric Depression: A Review of Evidence-Based Psychogenic Options," *Innovative Issues and Approaches in Social Sciences* (Vol. 8, No. 1:46-59, 2015).

"The Interpersonal Psychotherapy of Harry Stack Sullivan: Remembering the Legacy," *Journal of Psychology and Psychotherapy* (Volume 4, Issue 6, 2014).

"What to Do When There is Nothing to Do: The Psychotherapeutic Value of Meaning Therapy in the Treatment of Late Life Depression," *Health, Culture and Society,* Vol. 5, #1 (2013), pp.52-59.

"Late-Life Depression and the Counseling Agenda: Exploring Geriatric Logotherapy as a Treatment Modality," *International Journal of Psychological Research*, Vol. VI, #1 (2013).

"Geriatric Logotherapy: Exploring the Psychotherapeutics of Memory in Treating the Elderly," *Psychological Thought, Vol. 5, #2,* 2012:99-105.

"Pastoral Nurture of the Elderly: The 'Happy Memory' in Geriatric Logotherapy" in *Clinical Pastoral Psychotherapy: A Practitioner's Handbook for Ministry Professionals* Expanded 2nd Edition (Mishawaka, IN: GTF Books, 2012).

"Medication and Counseling in Psychiatric Practice: Biogenic Psychopharmacology and Psychogenic Psychotherapy (Partnering in the Treatment of Mental Illness)," in *Clinical Pastoral Psychotherapy: A Practitioner's Handbook for Ministry Professionals* (Expanded 2nd Edition, Mishawaka, IN: GTF Books, 2012).

"A Tribute to Carl Rogers," in Clinical Pastoral Psychotherapy: A Practitioner's Handbook for Ministry Professionals Expanded 2nd Edition (Mishawaka, IN: GTF Books, 2012).

"Psychology of Religion and the Books that Made it Happen," *Journal for the Study of Religions and Ideologies* Vol. X, #30 (2011), pp.277-298.

"*On Becoming a Person* (1961) Carl Rogers' Celebrated Classic in Memoriam," *Journal of Psychological Issues in Organizational Culture* (II, #3, 95-105, Oct. 2011).

"Ethical Naturalism in the Thought of E. O. Wilson: A Critical Review of His Major Works," *Journal for the Study of Religions and Ideologies* IX, 27 (Winter, 2010), 175-202.

"Harry Stack Sullivan and Interpersonal Psychotherapy: The Father of Modern Social Psychiatry," in *Foundation Theology 2010.*

"Personal Meaning as Psychotherapy: The Interpretive Hermeneutic of Viktor Frankl," in *Foundation Theology 2006.*

INTRODUCTION

Based on my professional assessment of the present state of theory and practice in psychotherapy as relates to the care and counseling of the post-retirement population in America, I have over the last few years concentrated much of my research and publishing in the field of geriatric psychotherapy. It is my conviction that the leading schools of psychotherapy, both classical and modern, have too quickly terminated their application and relevance to the growing number of post-retired individuals in need of pastoral care and counseling. The classical schools, it is understandable, were developed during a time when individuals did not live much beyond retirement age. The longevity of western populations during the time of Freud, Adler, Jung, and Frankl were not much beyond 65 years of age and even from Erikson the Sullivan, few Americans lived beyond 68 years with a small exceptional percentage. The development of psychotherapeutic theory and practice, therefore, addressed childhood, adolescent, young adulthood and family life, ending by and large with retirement. Even Erikson failed to move substantially into the post-retirement years and the psychopathology of the elderly.

However, it is my belief based on nearly 50 years of study, research, and teaching that even the modern schools – Horney, Klein, Perls, Berne, Maslow, Rogers, Fromm, Ellis, and Beck – have fallen victim to the inclination to too quickly terminate their theory and practice to these childhood-to-retirement categories and therefore, by default, have more or less failed to substantially address the post-retirement population which is rapidly and exponentially expanding. Indeed, whereas 50 years ago one expected to live a year or two beyond retirement, today a massive number of individuals living in western societies are living 20 to 30 years beyond retirement. The current schools of psychotherapy are finding themselves pressed to respond with theories and practices relevant to this population and, alas, too often they are coming up short with both theories and practices of value in the treatment of what I have chosen to call geriatric psychotherapy, i.e., psychotherapy developed specifically for the post-retirement population. The following 12 essays have been researched and published with the particular purpose of addressing this void in theory and practice. (Note: Though each has been previously published in peer-reviewed scholarly journals, they have been up-dated and adjusted to address the specific concerns and issues faced by ministry professionals involved in pastoral care and counseling related specifically to the post-retirement individual and community).

CHAPTER ONE

Palliative Psychotherapeutic Options in Geriatric Depression Management: Evidence-Based Non-Pharmacological Treatments in Review

Neither psychotherapeutic nor biological psychiatry has made a name for itself in developing new approaches to the treatment of depression among the palliative care patient community. However, what is now being called palliative care psychiatry is on the rise as an emerging subspecialty where palliative medicine and psychiatry converge (Fairman and Irwin, 2013). The interfacing of palliative care medicine with psychiatry is being heralded throughout the medical community as a positive step forward in the development of modalities of treatment, both pharmacologically-linked and psychotherapeutic, which may be further researched and evidence-based tested for efficacy.

The development of geriatric, late life, and post-retirement psychotherapies within the health care professions (Arean, Hegel, Vannoy, Fan, and Unutzer, 2008; Ayeers, Sorrell, Thorp, and Wetherell, 2007; Landreville, Laudry, Baillargeon, Guerette, and Mattewa, 2001) including, and of particular interest to us here, palliative psychotherapeutic care has in recent years become an increasingly important component of comprehensive health care treatment options. There are a large number of counselors and psychotherapists as well as psychiatrists, however, who find themselves with an increase in post-retirement clients and patients but without the benefit of specific training in treating this particular constituency (Karel, Ogland-Hand, Gatz, and Unuetzer, 2002; Gatz, Fiske, Fox, Kaskie, Kasl-Godley, and McCallum, 1999; Hinrichsen, 2008). There is a large population of older individuals in need of assistance in dealing with depression and its cognates of anxiety and self-esteem issues which are of particular concern to the health care profession working in palliative care medicine (Stanley, Wilson, Novy, Rhoades, Wagener, Greisinger, 2009; Knight and McCallum, 1998).

That there is a relative void in the training of palliative care health professionals in geriatric psychotherapy, particularly as relates to the treatment of depression, is very evident according to recent AMA-sponsored studies (Gallagher-Thompson and Steffen, 1994). In the following essay, we will delineate and discuss briefly evidence-based treatment options available to the counseling and psychotherapeutic community dealing particularly with palliative psychotherapeutic depression (Scogin and McElreath, 1994). As we know, biogenic depression calls for pharmacological intervention and, therefore, medical oversight. However, our interest here is rather to call attention to several proven modalities of treatment available for the non-medically trained psychotherapist dealing with palliative psychogenic depression (Knight and Qualls, 2006). There are several modalities of treatment for late-life depression for both institutionalized patients and those living at home (Francis and Kumar, 2013) including cognitive and behavioral therapy, problem-solving therapy, reminiscence and life review therapy, brief psychodynamic therapy, and interpersonal therapy. These studies are consistently showing evidence-based findings validating the use of each of these modalities of treatment of depression and depressive symptoms in older adults.

There are consistent evidence-based studies showing that non-pharmacological interventions offer the prospects of reducing cognitive decline in late life depression patients as well as the improvement of psychosocial aspects of older individuals suffering from mild cognitive impairment or Alzheimer's dementia (Herholz, Herholz, and Herholz, 2013). The absence of side effects owing to the non-pharmacological therapies employed make those therapies attractive options for the therapist, the patient, and the family involved. Recent studies will be reviewed here including those involving cognitive training and reminiscence and also such components as visual art and music, physical activities, and electromagnetic stimulation.

Specific treatment modalities which have an evidence-based effectiveness record to date include Cognitive Behavior Therapy (Barrowclough, King, Colville, Russell, Burns, and Tarrier, 2001; Cappeliez, 2001; Siskin, 2002), Brief Dynamic Therapy (Messer, 2001), Interpersonal Psychotherapy (Hinrichsen and Clougherty, 2006), Reminiscence Therapy (Bohlmeijer, Smit, and Cuijpers, 2003), and Geriatric Logotherapy (Morgan, 2012). These are commonly used by non-medically oriented psychotherapists and professional counselors in palliative health care facilities and, as will be indicated, have proven consistently to be effective tools for therapy in dealing with older clients as illustrated by evidence-based empirical studies (Arean and Ayalon, 2005).

Behavioral therapies, particularly Cognitive Behavioral Therapy (CBT) and Rational Emotive Behavior Therapy (REBT), have been the most used modalities of treating non-medical or psychogenic depression among older clients and have the largest data-base evidence for effectiveness (Floyd and Scogin, 1998). Depression is considered within the cognitive behavioral school of psychotherapy to essentially constitute the inability of the individual to cope with stress brought on by the aging process itself including such things as problem solving skills, isolation within the social matrix of daily living, and the decline in physical skills capabilities. The emphasis in these CBT treatment options focuses upon the practicalities of skill enhancement and the intentionality in the reorientation towards life stressors by reconfiguring the client's daily schedule, priorities, and inclinations (Gatz, 2007). CBT and its variants have proven very effective in facilitating the older client, post-retirement particularly, in redefining one's life situation, the *Sitz im Leben*, to accommodate a new understanding of one's relationship to the social environment of interpersonal relationships, life skills, and self-satisfaction. Evidence is strong for the overwhelming success of CBT compared to other modalities of depression treatment as well as wait-list controls and no treatment at all. And, this evidential data demonstrates that CBT has a longevity value beyond that of pharmacological treatments as well (Hyer, Hilton, Sacks, Freidman, and Yeager, 2009). The CBT agenda is two-fold, viz., to reduce the psychogenic depression and to elevate the social interaction and the physical skills-based functioning of the client. Reduction of depressive behavior while increasing social and physical activity constitutes the treatment agenda of CBT, and the evidence for its effectiveness is substantial.

It is generally agreed among health care workers that psychosocial factors constitute a significant component in the care and treatment of the elderly and recipients of palliative care. Up until just recently, however, data-based evidence of the effectiveness of the various treatment modalities has been absent or grossly under represented (Rodin, 2013). The consideration of significant developments in psychosocial research relative to this population as recipients of palliative care treatment modalities is crucial if continued development of effective care treatments are to be produced and refined. The various factors of methodological limitations, protective attitudes of health-care providers, and the progressive deterioration of patients with terminal disease have heretofore proven effective deterrents to evidence-based studies. Recently refined and improved valid and reliable measurements of various psychological features of distress and well-being has greatly improved the potential for producing evidence-based results in palliative care treatment of the elderly and terminally ill.

One area in which palliative care medical practice has only just begun to address itself is the realization that since half of cancer patients today continue to die of the disease, there is inevitably a persistence of psychological distress associated with it. Though not inevitably a death sentence, diagnosed cancer can and does produce emotional stress and often debilitating depression on the part of the patient though little research yet exists addressing this reality. An assessment of the work of the Japan Psycho-Oncology Society (Akechi, 2010) is relevant to this agenda particularly as relates to the psychiatric conditions produced within the diagnosed patient. Such patients frequently develop adjustment disorders and debilitating depression including anticipatory nausea and vomiting for patients receiving emetogenic chemotherapeutic agents. Common throughout the medical community is the awareness that terminally ill cancer patients inevitably prefer psychotherapeutic intervention rather than pharmacological therapy for the management of their depression. The amelioration of depression within the palliative care treatment patient using evidence-based effective psychotherapies constitutes the agenda for the health care giver and the institutional support team of medical personnel.

One of the great advances in the care and treatment of the end-of-life patient has been the rapid and substantial recognition on the part of medical personnel of the central importance of the psychological and social aspects of palliative care treatment (Pasacreta and Pickett, 1998). The acceleration of anxiety, distress, and depression occurs along the illness trajectory, and the psychological and social *milieu* within which the patient lives, institutionalized or at home, creates the potential for effective care based on an understanding of the attending physician, the care giver, and the family of these factors.

Studies (Connell, 1988) are now regularly providing evidence-based data to validate the effectiveness of Reminiscence Therapy (RT) used in the treatment of geriatric depression within the nursing home institutional setting. RT is a non-pharmacological intervention involving the prompting of past memories on the part of the palliative care patient. Clearly the most prevalent mental health disorder among institutionalized elderly is that of depression and Reminiscence Therapy. What is important in the Connell study is the use of RT "intermittently" rather than as the one primary modality of treatment employed once. Data is now showing that periodic, spaced, intermittent uses of RT have a greater evidence-based benefit.

Systematic assessment of the use of Reminiscence Therapy (RT) in the treatment of patients suffering from minor as well as major dementia (Dempsey, Murphy, Cooney, Casey, O'Shea, Devane, Jordan, and Hunter, 2014) reveals that there is currently no consistent definition of RT within the healthcare literature or professional practice though there is a consistency of characteristics of the various definitional parameters of the term and its usage. There is a characteristic divergence in the goals, theory base, and content of the competing definitional matrices of RT practice including the use of such terms as life review, early life events, remembered childhood relationships, etc. However, universally agreed upon components of RT include stages of life, age, life transitional events, attention span issues, recall ability over time, vocalizations including tunes, and remembered stress situations. These studies demonstrate the common useage of RT in the treatment of dementia care showing effective results in enhancement of self-esteem, improved communication skills, self-worth, personal identity and a sense of individuality.

To date, studies of meta-analysis focusing on psychosocial interventions have failed to address specific treatment of individual Behavioral and Psychological Symptoms of Dementia (BPSD) involving personalized interventions. Based on 641 care home and nursing home studies involving cluster randomized controlled trials as well as pre- and post-test studies (Testad, Corbett, Aarsland, Lexow, Fossey, Woods, and Ballard, 2014), good evidence supporting the use of Reminiscence Therapy in improving mood swings and a diminishment of agitation is being regularly and systematically found.

The benefits of Reminiscence Therapy (RT) for the improvement of the quality of life of individuals, both in and out of institutionalized care facilities, suffering from dementia has consistently produced evidence-based validation. However, the value of RT for care givers has yet to be researched and documented (Melunsky, Crellin, Dudzinski, Orrell, Wenborn, Poland, Woods, and Charlesworth, 2014). Based on a recent study of 18 family care givers involved in group sessions, the evidence for effectiveness in enhancing their skills in interacting with dementia patients proved inconclusive with the suggestion that further study is needed. Without further study and evidence-based findings, the suggestion is that there is little justification in the continuation of joint reminiscence groups in dementia care.

Owing to the acute adaptation difficulties of older individuals being institutionalized for palliative care, the emergence of depression and cognates including agitation, apathy, and the on-set of minor dementia symptoms as well as a diminishment of a feeling of general well-being is proving consistently evident in nursing home reports (Melendez-Moral, Charco-Ruiz, Mayordomo-Rodriguez, and Sales-Galan, 2013). Reminiscence Therapy (RT) has consistently proven to be among the most effective non-pharmacological intervention modalities of palliative care treatment with a minimum of debilitating side-effects while maximizing the reduction of these depressive symptoms.

In spite of the frequency of reports of effectiveness in the use of Reminiscence Therapy (RT) in the treatment of depression and dementia among the institutionalized elderly population (Klever, 2013), there is a conspicuous absence of actual research evidence addressing the specifics of the connection between reminiscence functions and the reduction of depressive symptoms (Hallford, Mellor, and Cummins, 2013). The Hallford and colleagues' study tests the hypothesis regarding the "indirect associations of adaptive integrative and instrumental reminiscence functions with depressive symptoms," addressing the question regarding whether or not these relationships might differ from younger to older patients. This study of 730 younger and 725 older individuals provided evidence-based validation of the effectiveness of RT in the treatment of both age groups in the reduction of depression and depressive symptoms including having substantive impacts upon meaning of life issues, self-esteem, and personal optimism about the future.

With both the rise of dementia and psychogenic depression among the over-65 year old population in the U.S. which continues to rise exponentially owing to the baby-boomers, there is evidence of an increasing need for more responsive evidence-based validated psychotherapeutic modalities of treatment. Reminiscence Therapy (RT) is proving to be one of those which is providing evidence-based validation of its effectiveness and is supplemented with the use of "technologies" as explored by Lazar and team (Lazar and Demiris, 2014). Such things as photographic artifacts as well as period-based music used in the facilitation of social interaction within group as well as individual treatment plans is gaining support within the counseling and psychotherapeutic communities. A diminishment of depression and a documented rise in self-esteem are two prevalent benefits of the use of these material supplements called Information and Communication Technologies (ICT). Another benefit documented in these evidence-based studies is that of patients actually taking ownership of conversations in both group settings and with one-on-one relationships with a family member, therapist, or care giver. The use of what are referred to as multimedia reminiscence materials also results, according to these studies, in the reduction of barriers to motor deficits in the interaction.

A specific study of male veterans (Chue and Chang, 2014) utilizing Group Reminiscence Therapy (GRT) was conducted in a nursing facility's intervention program evaluating 3-month and 6-month effects on depressive symptoms for institutionalized male veterans. Following a 4-week intervention, the evidence-based findings validated the effectiveness of this treatment plan based on reduced depressive symptoms. This increasingly popular variation on Reminiscence Therapy labeled Group Reminiscence Therapy (GRT) is commonly used within a group of age peers suffering from psychogenic depression in an institutional setting such as a residential nursing home. GRT functions as a brief and structured intervention and according to Gaggioli and colleagues (Gaggioli, Scaratti, Morganti, Stramba-Badiale, Agostoni, Spatola, Molinari, Cipresso, and Riva, 2014), it is proving with evidence-based demonstrations the increased effectiveness for group therapy beyond its already validated effectiveness with individuals.

Problem-Solving Therapy (PST) (Kiosses and Alexopoulos, 2014) is a component of the treatment of geriatric psychogenic depression and is consistently reporting an evidence-based effectiveness rate justifying both its continued use and further data-collection and assessment. PST has demonstrated empirically its effectiveness comparable to those studies using paroxetine and placebo treatment plans with patients suffering from minor depression as well as dysthymia. Its effectiveness has been further demonstrated in reducing symptoms of depression in undiagnosed patients. A particularly attractive feature of PST is that among stroke patients, for example, they were less likely to develop depressive episodes, both major and minor, than those who receive placebo treatment. One final and important finding was that PST patients had significantly lower 2-month incidence rates of major depression than those receiving usual institutional care and were less likely to develop apathy than placebo treated patients.

Meaning Centered Group Psychotherapy (MCGP) is also becoming increasingly recognized as a legitimate treatment modality addressing the spiritual and values-based worldview of the terminally ill and end-of-life elderly palliative care patient (Breithart, Rosenfeld, Gibson, Pessin, Poppito, Nelson, Tomarken, Timm, Berg, Jacobson, Sorger, Abbey, and Olden, 2010). Though begun gradually, the increased acceleration of the acceptance of MCGP by the medical and palliative care community has provided a new arena for the religiously oriented individual and family to seek out and respond to medical care and treatment which demonstrates a sensitivity to the worldview and ethos embodied in a faith-based patient's life. In a study reported by Breithhart and colleagues, there were 90 terminally ill patients who participated in an 8-week treatment intervention followed by another 8-week intervention two months later. Assessments included measuring spiritual well-being, meaning, hopelessness, desire for death, optimism/pessimism, anxiety, depression and overall quality of life. The evidence-based study showed a considerable improvement in the patient's sense of spiritual well-being and a sense of meaning to life with an even greater advancement in these feelings following the second intervention. However, there was no measurable improvement among individuals participating in the Supportive Group Psychotherapy (SGP) which led the researchers to suggest that more study of the efficacy of the MCGP approach to end-of-life palliative care should be aggressively pursued owing to the initial very positive findings.

Mindfulness-Based Supportive Therapy (MBST) is addressed particularly to palliative psychotherapy employed in the treatment of psycho-existential suffering of the end-of-life patient. MBST consists of five key components, viz., presence, listening, empathy, compassion, and boundary awareness. There is yet to be produced evidence-based efficacy of this newly emerging palliative care treatment therapy, but confidence is high among the developers of this new therapy sufficient to merit further data-base study (Beng, Chin, Guan, Yee, Wu, Jane, and Meng, 2013).

From its early inception, the goal of palliative care has been portrayed as "helping patients to die with dignity." The overall characterization of palliative care has to do with dignity of the patient as a framework for the attending physician, the patient, the care giver, and the family in determining the objectives and therapeutic considerations essential to end-of-life care (Chochinov, 2002). A term increasingly used in this arena is "dignity-conserving care" for it places the responsibility on the health care environment to foster specifically this goal. It constitutes both a treatment objective as well as a governing principle for the entire health care environment.

Dignity Therapy (DT) is a short-term palliative psychotherapy developed for patients living with a life-limiting illness. However, there continues to be a need for the demonstration of the effectiveness of DT in the treatment of depression and anxiety among the elderly and those in palliative care treatment. In this study (Juliao, Barbosa, Oliveira, Nunes, and VazCarneiro, 2013), 60 terminally ill individuals participated in the assessment of the value and efficacy of DT. The findings verified the short-term beneficial effects on depression and anxiety, and the data were sufficiently strong as to merit further study.

The use of Dignity Therapy is definitely on the rise in both institutional care facilities for the elderly and for the treatment of end-of-life palliative patients (Juliao, Olivera, Nunes, VazCarneiro, and Barbosa, 2014). It is a brief psychotherapeutic modality treatment for depression and anxiety for the institutionalized elderly with terminal illness where a high level of distress is evidenced by palliative caregivers. Based on a study of 80 patients, it was found that dignity therapy resulted in a measurable evidence-based beneficial effect on both depression and anxiety. Over a 30-day period, the therapeutic benefits were maintained and, based on the efficacy of dignity therapy, future trials of DT should be commenced and compared to other psychotherapeutic non-pharmacological approaches.

Existential Behavioral Therapy (EBT) was developed to support informal caregivers of palliative patients in the last stage of life and during bereavement as a manualized group psychotherapy (Febb, Brandstatter, Kogler, Hauke, Rechenberg-Winter, Fensterer, Kuchenhoff, Hentrich, Belka, and Borasio, 2013). Consisting of six sessions only, EBT was tested using 160 individuals for effectiveness in the treatment of mental stress and quality of life issues. The evidence-based study demonstrated an effective benefit in dealing with distress and anxiety as well as quality of life issues among caregivers of palliative patients. However, it must be emphasized that, given the uniqueness of the study and smallness of the sample, more study is required for conclusive validation of the early findings.

Even though palliative care is now considered an indispensable component of end-of-life care, there is still only a small amount of evidence-based effectiveness studies of its use assessing the efficacy of intervention-oriented treatments. There is one (Hansen, Enright, Baskin, and Klatt, 2009), called Forgiveness Therapy (FT) which is now beginning to provide evidence-based validation of its efficacy in improving psychological well-being on the part of the patient and promises to be a valuable component of terminal care treatment plans. Measuring such things as forgiveness, hope, quality of life, and anger issues, FT therapy groups consistently showed a measurable improvement in all areas tested sufficient to justify consideration as a standard treatment procedure in dealing with the terminally ill elderly.

Palliative psychotherapy is a fairly recent arrival in the care and treatment of the terminally ill and particularly geriatric institutionalized patients suffering from debilitating depression. Its rapid success in evidence-based effectiveness has inevitably insinuated its utility and value into the overall treatment of geriatric depression. What we have done here is to review some of the more successful and recently developed treatment modalities in palliative psychotherapy of geriatric depression patients, calling attention to the proliferation of evidence-based effectiveness studies and identifying those methodologies which are still in need of further development and effectiveness verification. In the meantime, palliative psychotherapy in the treatment of geriatric depression is a growing field of specialization, and it continues to justify its place in the overall treatment plan of institutionalized elder care.

REFERENCES

Akechi, T. (2010). "Essential Psychological Care in Palliative Medicine." *Psychiatria et Neurologia Japanica,* 112 (10):1029-1035.

Arean, P., Hegel, M., Vannoy, S., Fan, M. Y. & Unutzer, J. (2008). "Effectiveness of Problem-Solving Therapy for Older, Primary Care Patients with Depression: Results from the IMPACT Project," *The Gerontologist,* 48(3), 311-323.

Arean, P., & Ayalon, LO. (2005). "Assessment and Treatment of Depressed Older Adults in Primary Care," *Clinical Psychology: Science and Practice,* 12(3), 321-335.

Ayeers, C. R., Sorrell, J. T., Thorp, S. R., & Wetherell, J. L. (2007). "Evidence-Based Psychological Treatments for Late-Life Anxiety," *Psychology and Aging,* 22(1), 8-17.

Barrowclough, C., King, P.., Colville, J., Russell, E., Burns, A., & Tarrier, N. (2001). "A randomized Trial of the Effectiveness of Cognitive-Behavioral Therapy and Supportive Counseling for Anxiety Symptoms in Older Adults," *Journal of Consulting & Clinical Psychology,* 69)5), 756-762.

Beng, T. S., Chin, L. E., Guan, N. C., Yee, A., Wu, C., Jane, L. E., and Meng, C. B. (2013). "Mindfulness-Based Supportive Therapy (MBST): Proposing a Palliative Psychotherapy From a Conceptual Perspective to Address Suffering in Palliative Care. " *American Journal of Hospital Palliative Care,* October 21 (pre-released citation).

Breithart, W., Rosenfeld, B., Gibson, C., Pessin, H., Poppito, S., Nelson, C., Tomarken, A., Timm, A. K., Berg, A., Jacobson, C., Sorger, B., Abbey, J., and Olden, M. (2010). "Meaning-Centered Group Psychotherapy for Patients with Advanced Cancer: A Pilot Randomized Controlled Trial," *Psycho-Oncology,* 19 (1), 21-8.

Cappeliez, P. (2001). "Presentation of Depression and Response to Group Cognitive Therapy with Older Adults," *Journal of Clinical Geropsychology,* 6(3), 165-174.

Chochinov, H. M. (2002). "Dignity-Conserving Care--A New Model for Palliative Care: Helping the Patient Feel Valued." *Journal of the American Medical Association,* 287 (17):2253.

Chueh, K. H. and Chang, T. Y. (2014). "Effectiveness of Group Reminiscence Therapy for Depression Symptoms in Male Veterans: 6-Month Follow-Up." *International Journal of Geriatric Psychiatry.* April, 29(4):377-383.

Connell, P. (1988). "The Effects of Intermittent Reminiscence Therapy on Nursing Home Residents' Depression Levels," (Paper presented at the Annual Meeting of the American Society on Aging (34th, San Diego, CA, March 18-22).

Dempsey, L., Murphy, K., Cooney, A., Casey, D., O'Shea, E., Devane, D., Jordan, F., and Hunter, A. (2014). "Reminiscence in Demintia: A Concept Analysis." *Dementia (London)* March, 1;13(2):176-92.

Fairman, N., and Irwin, S. A. (2013). "Palliative Care Psychiatry: Update on an Emerging Dimension of Psychiatric Practice." *Current Psychiatry Reports,* July, 15(7):374.

Febb, M. J., Brandstatter, M., Kogler, M., Hauke, G., Rechenberg-Winter, P., Fensterer, V., Kuchenhoff, H., Hentrich, M., Belka, C., and Borasio, G. D. (2013). "Existential Behavioural Therapy for Informal Caregivers of Palliative Patients: A Randomized Controlled Trial." *Psychooncology,* September, 22(9):2079-2086.

Floyd, M., & Scogin, F. (1998). "Cognitive-Behavior Therapy for Older Adults: How Does it Work?," *Psychotherapy,* 35(4), 459-463.

Francis, J. L. and Kumar, A. (2013). "Psychological Treatment of Late-Life Depression." *Psychiatric Clinics of North America,* Dec, 36(4):561-75.

Gaggioli, A., Scaratti, C., Morganti, L., Stramba-Badiale, M., Agostoni, M., Spatola, C.A., Molinari, E., Cipresso, P., and Riva, G. (2014). "Effectiveness of Group Reminiscence for Improving Wellbeing of Institutionalized Elderly Adults: Study Protocol for a Randomized Controlled Trial." *Trials,* Oct. 25, 15(1):408.

Gallagher-Thompson, D., & Steffen, A. M. (1994). "Comparative Effects of Cognitive
Behavioral and Brief Psychodynamic Psychotherapies for Depressed Family Caregivers,
Journal of Consulting and Clinical Psychology, 62(3), 543-549.

Gatz, M. (2007). "Commentary on Evidence-Based Psychological Treatments for Older Adults," *Psychology and Aging,* 22(1), 52-55.

Hallford, D. J., Mellor, D., and Cummins, R. A. (2013). "Adaptive Autobiographical Memory in Younger and Older Adults: The Indirect Association of Integrative and Instrumental Reminiscence with Depressive symptoms." *Memory,* 21(4):444-457.

Hansen, M. J., Enright, R.D., Baskin, T. W., and Klatt, J. (2009). "A Palliative Care Intervention in Forgiveness Therapy for Elderly Terminally Ill Cancer Patients." *Journal of Palliative Care*, 25 (1), 51-60.

Herholz, S. C., Herholz, R. S., and Herholz, K. (2013). "Non-Pharmacological Interventions and Neuroplasticity in Early Stage Alzheimer's Disease." *Expert Review of Neurotherapeutics,* Nov., 13(11)1235-1245.

Hinrichsen, G. A., & Clougherty, K. F. (2006). *Interpersonal Psychotherapy for Depressed Older Adults.* Washington, D.C.: American Psychological Association.

Hyer, L., Hilton, N., Sacks, A., Freidman, M., & Yeager, C. (2009). "GIST: An Efficient and Effective Cognitive Behavioral Therapy in Long Term Care," *American Journal of Alzheimer's Disease and Other Dementias,* 23 (6), 528-539.

Juliao, M., Barbosa, A., Oliveira, F., Nunes, B., and Vaz Carneiro, A. (2013). "Efficacy of Dignity Therapy for Depression and Anxiety in Terminally Ill Patients: Early Results of a Randomized Controlled Trial." *Palliative Support Care,* December, 11(6):481-489.

Juliao, M., Oliveira, F., Nunes, B., Vaz Carneiro, A., and Barbosa, A. (2014). "Efficacy of Dignity Therapy on Depression and Anxiety in Portuguese Terminally Ill Patients: A Phase II Randomized Controlled Trial." *Journal of Palliative Medicine,* June, 17(6):688-695.

Karel, M. J., Hinrichsen, G. (2000). "Treatment of Depression in Late Life: Psychotherapeutic Interventions," *Clinical Psychology Review* 20(6):707-729.

Kiosses, D.N. and Alexopoulos, G.S. (2014). "Problem-Solving Therapy in the Elderly." *Current Treat Options Psychiatry* March, 1(1):15-26.

Klever, S. (2013). "Reminiscence Therapy: Finding Meaning in Memories." *Nursing,* April, 43(4):36-37.

Kogleer, M., Brandl, J., Brandstatter, M., Borasio, G.D., and Fegg, M.J. (2013). "Determinants of the Effect of

Existential Behavioral Therapy for Bereaved Partners: A Qualitative Study," *Journal of Palliative Medicine,* 16 (11), 1410-1416.

Knight, B. G., & McCallum, T. J. (1998). "Adapting Psychotherapeutic Practice for Older Clients: Implications of the Contextual, Cohort-Based, Maturity, Specific Challenge Model," *Professional Psychology: Research & Practice,* 29(1), 15-22.

Knight, B. G. & Qualls, S. H. (2006). *Psychotherapy for Depression in Older Adults.* New York: John Wiley & Sons, Inc.

Landreville, P., Laudry, J., Baillargeon, L., Guerette, A., & Matteau, E. (2001). "Older Adults' Acceptance of Psychological and Pharmacological Treatments for Depression," *Journal of Gerontology: Psychological Sciences,* 56B, 285-291.

Lazar, A., Thompson, H., and Demiris, G. (2014). "A Systematic Review of the Use of Technology for Reminiscence Therapy." Oct., 41(1 Suppl):51S-61S.

Meléndez-Moral, J.C., Charco-Ruiz, L., Mayordomo-Rodríguez, T., and Sales-Galán, A. (2013). "Effects of a Reminiscence Program Among Institutionalized Elderly Adults." *Psicothema,* 25(3):319-23.

Melunsky, N., Crellin, N., Dudzinski, E., Orrell, M., Wenborn, J., Poland, F., Woods, B., and Charlesworth, G. (2014). "The Experience of Family Carers Attending a Joint Reminiscence Group with People with Dementia: A Thematic Analysis." *Dementia (London),* April, 13(3): 49-78.

Messer, S.B. (2001). "What Makes Brief Psychodynamic Therapy Time Efficient?" *Clinical Psychology* 8(1):5-22.

Morgan, John H. (1987). *From Freud to Frankl: Our Modern Search for Personal Meaning.* Bristol, IN: Wyndham Hall Press.

Morgan, John H. (2010). *Clinical Pastoral Psychotherapy: A Practitioner's Handbook for Ministry Professionals.* South Bend, IN: GTF Books.

Morgan, John H. (2012a). "Geriatric Logotherapy: Exploring the Psychotherapeutics of Memory in Treating the Elderly," *Psychological Thought, Vol. 5, #2,* pp. 99-105.

Morgan, John H. (2012b). *Beginning With Freud: The Classical Schools of Psychotherapy* (Expanded 2nd Edition). Lima, OH: Wyndham Hall Press

Morgan, John H. (2014a). *After Freud: The Modern Schools of Psychotherapy .* South Bend, IN: GTF Books.

Pasacreta, J.V. and Pickett, M. (1998). "Psychosocial Aspects of Palliative Care." *Seminars in Oncology Nursing,* 14 (2):110-120.

Rodin, Gary (2013). "Research on Psychological and Social Factors in Palliative Care: An Invited Commentary." *Palliative Medicine,* 27 (10), 925-31.

Scogin, F., & McElreath, L. (1994). "Efficacy of Psychosocial Treatments for Geriatric Depression: A

Quantitative Review," *Journal of Consulting and Clinical Psychology,* 62(1), 69-74.

Siskin, L. P. (2002). "Cognitive-Behavioral Therapy with Older Adults," *Behavior Therapist,* 25(1), 3-6.

Stanley, M. A., Wilson, N. L., Novy, D. M., Rhoades, H. M., Wagener, P. D., Greisinger, A. J., & et al. (2009). "Cognitive Behavior Therapy for Generalized Anxiety Disorder Among Older Adults in Primary Care: A Randomized Clinical Trial," *The Journal of the American Medical Association,* 301(14), 146-1467.

Testad, I., Corbett, A., Aarsland, D., Lexow, K.O., Fossey, J., Woods, B., and Ballard, C. (2014). "The Value of Personalized Psychosocial Interventions to Address Behavioral and Psychological Symptoms in People with Dementia Living in Care Home Settings: A Systematic Review." *International Psychogeriatrics,* July, 26(7):1083-98.

CHAPTER TWO
The Interpersonal Psychotherapy of Harry Stack Sullivan: Remembering the Legacy

Just a little over sixty years ago (January 14, 1949), Harry Stack Sullivan died of a persistent cardiovascular disease while attending an international conference, the World Federation for Mental Health, in Paris where his life's work was being critically and enthusiastically touted as a major contribution to a deepening understanding of psychotherapy in the modern world. Following in the wake of Freud, Jung, and Adler, Sullivan stepped forward with both an appreciation of the psychoanalytic tradition and a readiness and willingness to reach across disciplines to the social and behavioral sciences to deepen his understanding of the complexities of mental illness as related to interpersonal relationships and particularly to schizophrenia. This willingness to venture out has resulted in Sullivan being acclaimed by many as the "father of modern psychiatry" (Perry, 1987; Mullahy, 1970; Mullahy, 1973) and by others as an interdisciplinary innovator worthy of international acclaim in mental health treatment (Lundin, 1985).

Born of poor Irish Catholic farming parents in upper New York State in February, 1892, amidst many Protestants and few Catholics, Sullivan had no siblings and lived a solitary life and a precocious child until the age of sixteen when he enrolled in Cornell University with a State scholarship in 1908. "Brilliant and taciturn" as he was, his ambition drove him to successfully seek admission into the chartered, but somewhat dubious, Chicago College of Medicine and Surgery in 1911 where general medicine was the curriculum with no psychiatry to be found.

Gaining the medical diploma in 1917, he bounced around from one hospital to another where, by sheer dent of determination, he worked with the mentally ill patients, and particularly schizophrenics, employing a method he early on labeled "interpersonal therapy." Two years in medical practice with the U.S. Army landed him a position at the prestigious St. Elizabeth's Hospital in Washington, D.C., where, without any previous training in psychiatry other than what he had taught himself, he was invited to work with the notable Freudian psychiatrist, William Alanson White, M.D. Whether it was the luck of the Irish or his own tenacity and self-confidence, Sullivan was also made a clinical researcher at Sheppard and Enoch Pratt Hospital and subsequently named to the faculty of the University of Maryland's School of Medicine.

During what he in later years looked back on as his "Baltimore period," he began to research, write, and speak about his therapeutic treatment of the mentally ill, particularly schizophrenia, and thereby built a reputation which resulted in his being called to the Washington School of Psychiatry as staff faculty and chairman of the Council of Fellows and editor of the School's internationally distinguished journal, *Psychiatry.* As with other great innovators in the sciences, Sullivan's fortuitous and profoundly beneficial acquaintances with some of the leading social scientists of the day became the basis upon which he furthered his interest in interpersonal relationships as a key to mental health (Hall and Lindzey, 1957). Such collegial associates as Edward Sapir, a cultural anthropologist and Harold Lasswell, a political scientist, of the University of Chicago wielded great influence upon Sullivan's interest in the behavioral sciences, as did his personal acquaintances with George Herbert Mead, Robert Ezra Park, and W. I. Thomas, the internationally distinguished sociologists of the time all teaching at the University of Chicago. Finally, in New York City where he had established a very successful private practice, his friendships with the outstanding psychologists of the day, Erich Fromm, Frieda Fromm-Reichmann, and Adolf Meyer proved crucial to his final developmental stages of theory-building (Kendler, 1987).

In 1939, the William Alanson White Foundation decided that a series of lectures should be given to honor the memory of White, a colleague of Sullivan's, who had died in 1937, and, of course, Sullivan was chosen to give the first series. He actually gave five lectures to an enthusiastic group of professionals in an auditorium owned by the Department of the Interior in Washington, DC. In these lectures, Sullivan made his first public attempt to present both a comprehensive and well-thought-out explanation of his concept of personality development including psychiatric disorders and treatment. In February of 1940, they were all published in the journal, *Psychiatry*, at the insistence of Sullivan's friends and colleagues, but against his best judgment. He was not pleased with his performance but finally consented and they appeared. Not surprisingly, they attracted much attention within the psychiatric and social science communities and in the following years many mental health and social science professional workers wrote to secure copies of this issue of the periodical. Finally, in 1947, much to the chagrin of Sullivan who believed his presentation of his thoughts was "grossly inadequate," a new printing of these lectures came out again in *Psychiatry*. This was a hardback edition and carried the somewhat dubious title of *Conceptions of Modern Psychiatry* (Sullivan, 1953a). This was actually his only book, at least in his lifetime, to see the light of day though several subsequent volumes of his lectures and essays, all touted to be Sullivan's books and finally appeared. This one, however, sold 13,000 copies over the next several years and the William Alanson White Foundation gained considerable attention because of them. Under the same title, this book was published again four years after the death of Sullivan and it still sells well today. Sullivan, however, denounced many of the premature conceptual developments in the work and discounted its value.

Nevertheless, it is a pivotal work for our consideration and a few remarks are justified before we move to the fundamental concepts and theories of Sullivan's notions of personality. "Psychiatry," Sullivan wrote, "is the study of processes that involve or go on between people. The field of psychiatry is the field of interpersonal relations, under any and all circumstances in which these relations exist" (Sullivan, 1953a). This is the thesis set forth by Sullivan in this book. It is the first place where he expressed the central ideas of his theory of personality. Through his development of the theory, he made not only a vital contribution in the treatment of mental disorder -- in particular, schizophrenia (Sullivan, 1962) -- but he opened an entirely new approach to the study of human personality (Sullivan, 1953b). In the view of many analysts, he made the most original contribution to psychiatry since Freud. Rollo May has gone on record as saying, "As Freud was the prophet for the Victorian age of sexual suppression, Sullivan is the prophet for our schizoid age -- our age of unrelatedness, in which, beneath all the chatter of radio and newspapers and all the multitudes of 'contact,' people are often strangers to each other" (Perry, 1982).

In this work, he created a new viewpoint which is known today as the "interpersonal theory of psychiatry." Sullivan's fundamental emphasis related to a theory of personality which is a "relatively enduring pattern of recurrent interpersonal situations which characterize a human life" (Sullivan, 1953b). Radically shifting from the psychoanalytic focus on the unconscious, Sullivan brought to his clinical research and practice a behavioral and social science perspective which had not been considered a significant component of personality theory until he did it (Sullivan, 1964). He argued that the concept of "personality" is itself a hypothetical entity which cannot be isolated from interpersonal situations and, indeed, interpersonal behavior is all that is observable about personality. The rest, he suggests, is strictly metaphorical speculation and creative imagery. It is futile and fruitless to speak of a person's personality outside the social interactive matrix of the living person. Not discounting the significance of heredity and the maturation process as affected by the physical environment, the real thing that determines the nature of a human person is the social interaction of that person with others (Sullivan, 1962).

Never before had such an attempt been made to merge psychiatry and social psychology (Millon, 1983). His theory of personality is the product of such a merger and it is greatly enriched by his acquaintance with and utilization of the social sciences. He writes: "The general science of psychiatry seems to me to cover much the same field as that which is studied by social psychology, because scientific psychiatry has to be defined as the study of interpersonal relations, and this in the end calls for the use of the kind of conceptual framework that we now call *field theory*. From such a standpoint, personality is taken to be hypothetical. That which can be studied is the pattern of processes which characterize the interaction of personalities in particular recurrent situations or fields which include the observer" (Sullivan, 1964). This attitude about the place and relevance of the "observer" in the clinical situation became a benchmark of Sullivan's innovative approach to the therapeutic encounter. He was, of course, influenced by the science philosopher, Heisenberg, on this point particularly (Amada, 1985).

Modern psychiatry, as defined and practiced by Sullivan, consists of a study of personality characteristics which can be directly observed in the context of interpersonal relationships (Sullivan, 1956). Systems of psychiatry based on statements about what is going on in the patient's mind are therefore similar to a system of thought which is built on axioms such as "All events are controlled by Divine Providence." The truth or falsehood of this statement cannot be established by things that reasonably well educated people can see, hear, and feel. Much human experience can be cited to support such a statement, and much human experience can be cited to nullify it, but it is so set up that it must always remain a matter of faith. For Sullivan, a "personality characteristic" is defined as the things which people can see, hear, and feel in their relationships with other individuals. This is the most fundamental working hypothesis in his personality theory (Sullivan, 1954).

Though Sullivan is only willing to allow personality to be purely hypothetical apart from the actually observable reality of social interaction, he does assert that it is a dynamic center of various processes which occurs in a series of interpersonal fields. This "dynamism" is a key concept in his overall personality theory (Sullivan, 1972). He gives significant place to these processes by identifying and naming them as he constructs a platform of their characteristics. These processes, then, are *dynamisms*, *personifications*, the *self-system*, and *cognitive processes*. Let's explore each briefly here as they constitute the backbone of his major work, *Conceptions of Modern Psychiatry* (Sullivan, 1953a).

The smallest unit of study in interpersonal relationships is what he calls "dynamism" (Sullivan, 1953b). It constitutes an energy transference which means any unit of behavior, either actual act or mental experience. These become habitual ways of acting which involve the physical body of the person, such as the mouth, hands, arms, legs, etc. These dynamisms can then be broken down into a plethora of subsets, such as the fear dynamism, intimate dynamism, etc. the dynamisms which are distinctively human in character are those which characterize one's interpersonal relations and function primarily to satisfy some basic needs of the individual. Three major dynamisms are malevolence, lust, and intimacy. Malevolence is the driving dynamism that one is living among one's own personal enemies and, if this negative dynamism emerges early in a child's life, he may find it difficult ever in adulthood to reach a fully trusting relationship with another person. Sullivan expressed it poignantly: "Once upon a time everything was love, but that was before I had to deal with people" (Sullivan, 1953a). Lust is another driving dynamism of the individual. Lust for Sullivan consists of the complex urges, feelings, and interpersonal actions which have genital sexual activity as their distant or immediate goal and lust begins in early adolescence. Sullivan rejected the Freudian concept of sexuality and suggested that it was more or less inconsequential in childhood and early adolescence, but lust constitutes a major driving force in later adolescence. Intimacy for Sullivan is a profoundly positive dynamism potentially. It occurs when the well-being of another person is as important to an individual as his own well-being. It does not occur in parent-child relationships and does not involve lust or sexual behavior. It occurs only between members of the same sex. Lust becomes, then, a "contaminant of intimacy" for lust seeks to serve itself rather than the other person.

Personifications consist of an image that an individual has of himself or of some other person. It is a complex of feelings, attitudes, and conceptions that grows out of experience with need-satisfaction and anxiety and, for example, Sullivan speaks often of the "good-mother," "bad-mother," and "overprotective mother" as examples (Sullivan, 1956). When these personifications are shared by a large social grouping, they become stereotypes such as "all Irishman are drunks," "all Catholics lie," etc., and these stereotypes are held by social groups without experience of their reality but of a shared personification of imagined behavior among peoples not personally known.

The self-system is another dynamism which is crucial to personality structure. It functions as a security measure to protect the individual from anxiety. In order to avoid or minimize actual or potential anxiety, the person adopts various types of protective measures and supervisory controls over his behavior. These security measures form the self-system which sanctions certain forms of behavior, such as the "good-me" self, and forbids other forms of behavior, such as the "bad-me" self.

Sullivan's unique contribution to the role of cognition in personality theory has to do with his development of a threefold classification of experiences, for, says he, experiences occur in three different modes -- *protaxic, parataxic, and syntaxic* (Sullivan, 1953b). These experiential modes merit a brief description in order to appreciate their relevance to Sullivan's interpersonal relations' description of psychiatry. Sometimes called "types of experience" and sometimes called "types of cognition," this tripartite foundation of personality encounters are worthy of close attention.

The simplest and most fundamental mode of experiencing reality at the beginning of life is what Sullivan chose to call the *prototoxic* mode. It consists of essentially a flowing of sensations, feelings, and images without any necessary connection between them, a kind of "stream of consciousness," if you will. Sullivan himself describes it this way: "It may be regarded as the discrete series of momentary states of the sensitive organism" (Sullivan, 1953b). It occurs, of course, during the earliest months of infancy and must precede the others as a preparation for them. The *parataxic* mode of thinking, Sullivan explains, consists of seeing causal relationships between events that occur at about the same time but which are not logically related. Getting the connection wrong is what this mode of experience is all about. It is magical thinking, says he, for there is no logical connection between two events experienced by the child in which the child assumes there is. It is essentially the "elementary externalization of causality." In childhood it occurs regularly when the child assumes that something he has done is the cause of something that is quite decidedly unrelated but he thinks it is. In adulthood, the residuals of parataxis modes of experiencing occur in such things as the presumed relationship between "praying hard" and "getting well."

Finally, the third and most advanced mode of experience is called *syntaxic* and it corresponds to logical, analytical thought. Syntaxic experience of reality thus presupposes the ability to understand physical and spatial causality, and the ability to predict causes from knowledge of their effects. The meaning of words and the use of numbers constitute the most poignant examples of the function of syntaxic experience and when the child learns the meaning of specific words and their uses and the nature of numbers and how they work, the child has reached this level of experiential sophistication needed in the development of interpersonal relationships.

Harry Stack Sullivan's distinguishing contribution to contemporary psychiatry was his heavy emphasis upon the social factors which contribute to the development of human personality (Hjelle and Ziegler, 1976). Though schooled in Freudian psychoanalysis, he was not a traditional Freudian for he differed from Freud in viewing the significance of the early parent-child relationship as being an early quest for security rather than, as in classical psychoanalysis, primarily sexual in origin and nature.

Drawing from his own personal life's story, Sullivan saw this child-mother relationship as central, not the sexual drive of libidinal instincts. Sullivan was intent upon integrating the multiple disciplines of the behavioral and social sciences into the work of psychiatry such that sociology and social psychology in the tradition of George Herbert Mead and Charles Horton Cooley proved most helpful in Sullivan's eventual development of what became known as interpersonal psychiatry, later interpersonal psychotherapy (Sullivan, 1964). He was not averse to reaching across disciplinary lines for theory and method, from evolution to communications, from learning theory to social organization. It was "interpersonal relations" which, he believed, constituted the fundamental ingredient in the personality structure.

Sullivan was averse to that form of psychiatry and clinical psychotherapy which dealt with mental illness through the study of institutionally-isolated patients. He had extensive experience in working with the mentally ill, particularly with schizophrenics, and he felt the institutionally committed constituted a weak source of clinical insight (Sullivan, 1962). Personality characteristics, for instance, he felt were determined by the interpersonal relationships between therapists and patients and that the institutional environment was artificial and counterproductive. Sullivan contended that personality develops according to people's perception of how others view them. "Others," in Sullivan thought, included personifications, like the government, as well as imaginary and idealized figures like Jesus or Moses or even movie stars. He believed, based upon his own clinical encounters with severely mentally ill patients, that cultural forces were largely responsible for their psychological condition (Sullivan, 1972). He contended that a healthy personality is the result of healthy relationships and that most of what goes in our society as mental illness is not "biogenic," but rather "sociogenic." Sullivan refused to employ the concept of "personality" as a unique, individual, and unchanging entity as so often was the case with traditionalists. He much preferred to define personality as a manifestation of the interaction between individuals, namely, interpersonal relations (Sullivan, 1953b).

Sullivan's clinical work in a variety of settings

through several years of medical assignments led him to believe firmly in the impact interpersonal relationships have upon personality development. He noted that individuals tend to carry distorted views and unrealistic expectations of others into their relationships. His solution was to become, as a clinical psychotherapist, a "participant observer" in dealing with his clients, taking a more active therapeutic stance than the traditional psychoanalytic "blank screen" approach popular at the time, particularly with traditional psychoanalysis. By focusing upon what he called "interpersonal behavior," he would observe the client's reaction to the therapist and the therapeutic environment. He believe that emotional well-being could be achieved by making an individual "aware" of their dysfunctional interpersonal patterns of interaction and thereby grow into a healthy self-awareness of their interactive behavior.

Before we consider Sullivan's now paradigmatic stages of personality development, we should say something about his concept of human nature and, it has been suggested by him many times, it can be summed up in the expression, "everyone is much more simply human than otherwise" (Sullivan, 1953a). Having made this his standard operational modality, he utilized it throughout his career and summed up its meaning this way: "In other words, the differences between any two instances of human personality from the lowest grade imbecile to the highest-grade genius -- are much less striking than the difference between the least-gifted human being and a member of the nearest other biological genus." Sullivan was outspoken on this point.

Denying that there were any really operative instincts left in the human person, and thus separating himself profoundly from the classical school of psychoanalysis, Sullivan contended that it is the social environment in which we mature that determines the effectiveness of our maturation. Interpersonal relationships are the essence of human development. We are only human in so far as we develop within the context of other people. We need to learn to compete, cooperate, and compromise with others as we mature in order to maintain mental health. He concluded, therefore, that personal individuality is an illusion. We exist only in relationship to other people. When we mature within a healthy social environment, this positive progression of interpersonal events leads to an integrated personality, to an adult who is capable of establishing satisfying interpersonal relations and who is able to both give and receive love. This is the essence of the human personality.

Sullivan's elaborate and well-developed description of the stages of human development were reminiscent of Freud's schematic system. But, whereas Freud built his developmental scheme around the central core of childhood sexuality, Sullivan built his around the fundamental core of interpersonal relationships. There are seven developmental stages in his schema and we will just mention them briefly here before concluding with remarks about his therapeutic method. Infancy is from the beginning to about eighteen months and the first expressions of the "self- system" appear when the infant encounters and relates to the "good me", "bad me" feeding experience in relationship to his mother. Childhood commences with the acquisition of language and goes through the preschool years. Syntaxic experience develops and the child encounters and deals with the reality and necessity of living with others as peers and authority figures. The juvenile person corresponds to the grade school years to about age eleven and here interpersonal relations includes competition, cooperation, and comprise as developmental necessities. Preadolescence is short, eleven to thirteen more or less, and here intimacy emerges in relationship to same-sex peers and chums and marks the first real instance of what Sullivan calls "genuine human relations." Early adolescence commences the heterosexual years of stress and physical development and the intimacy dynamic is matched with lust and lasts through the beginning of the high school years when late adolescence produces the profound demands of complex interpersonal relationships and particularly heterosexual ones fraught with anxiety. Adulthood arrives with the composite of strengths and weaknesses in the personality which has developed through the interpersonal experiences of the maturing process.

Sullivan's psychotherapeutic methodology was quite unique to his own understanding of the function and nature of interpersonal relationships. Sullivan firmly believed, based upon his extensive clinical experience, that mental disorders derive from interpersonal failures and, therefore, therapeutic procedures must be based upon a genuine effort to improve the patient's relationship skills in dealing with others (Sullivan, 1956). In keeping with his overall worldview, he believed that interpersonal relationships constitute the core of psychotherapeutic treatment. In this situation, it is imperative that the therapist understand that his role is primarily that of a "participant observer," for, despite all protestations to the contrary from traditionalists, the therapist becomes necessarily part of an interpersonal, face-to-face relationship with the patient. This process actually creates the opportunity for the patient to establish a syntaxic communication with another person, namely, the therapist himself.

Because of the emphasis upon the therapeutic role being that of an "observer," the therapist is exempt from becoming "involved" with the patient but, as with the Freudian tradition, the therapist must establish a relationship based upon his role as an expert in relationships, not just a friend, chum, or colleague. Unlike the work of Carl Rogers, Sullivan is insistent that the therapist "not" become a friend of the patient, thereby destroying the "observational" character of the therapist's relationship to the patient.

Sullivan had three primary objectives in the therapeutic situation (Sullivan, 1954). First, he intends to help the patient improve foresight, discover difficulties in interpersonal relations, and restore the ability to participate in consensually validated experiences. This occurs when three questions are addressed: (1) How can I best put into words what I wish to say to the patient, (2) What is the general pattern of communication between us, and (3) What precisely is the patient saying to me. Simplistic? Certainly not!

The therapeutic interview is divided into four stages: (1) formal inception, (2) reconnaissance, (3) detailed inquiry, and (4) termination. Let's explicate just briefly the character of each stage. At the first meeting, the psychiatrist promotes confidence in the patient by demonstrating interpersonal skills and permit's the patient to express the reasons for seeking therapy in the first place. The therapist, then, formulates tentative hypotheses regarding the declared cause for seeking treatment, and then decides on a possible course of action.

During reconnaissance, there is a general personal and social history established of the patient and the therapist who attempts to determine why the patient came to develop a particular personality type. Here, the therapist asks specific questions about the patient's age, birth order, mother, father, education, occupational history, marriage, children, etc. Open ended questions are asked to invite the patient to feel free to express the patient's emotional state at the time. Then, the detailed inquiry attempts to improve upon the therapist's understanding of the patient and the patient's understanding of the patient's own situation, particularly articulating why the patient has sought therapy. The fourth and final stage of the interview is termination, or, in some cases, interruption. Of course, this means that the interview has come to an end. Quite commonly, the therapist gives the client "homework," something to do or some memory to recall for the next session. After each session, the therapist makes copious notes about the session, what progress has been made and what issues have arisen that need addressing in the next session. For Sullivan, the therapeutic ingredient in this process is the face-to-face relationship between psychiatrist and patient, which permit's the patient to reduce anxiety and to communicate with others on the syntaxic level.

From Freud to Sullivan is not only a monumental leap in time but a quantitative leap in personality theory and psychotherapeutic theories of practice (Zeig, 1987). From the birth of Freud in 1856 to the death of Sullivan in 1949, the world of psychology and the practice of both psychiatry and psychotherapy have undergone a development comparable to that in biology and physics in the last hundred years. From Freud's fascination with the possibilities of exploring the "unconscious" of a patient through the use of dream interpretation, word associations, and hypnosis to Sullivan's clinically-demonstrated insight into the fundamental nature of interpersonal relationships skills as the determiner of mental health, one can argue that the discipline of psychology has remade itself. From deterministic behaviorism to the Third Force is no easy leap and with the initial and somewhat overpowering influence of the "depth" psychologists, Freud and Jung, the gradual emergence of the humanistic school of psychotherapy under the leadership of such clinical practitioners as Maslow, Frankl, and Rogers is nothing short of profound (Feist, 1985).

Interpersonal psychotherapy arrived upon the scene just when it seemed that "depth" psychology of the psychoanalytic type was waning in terms of both interest in and viability for those in the diverse fields of counseling. Certainly the arrival of Viktor Frankl's "will to meaning" followed by the humanistic Third Force movement has reinvigorated counseling psychology like no previous theoretical development in the history of the field. Not only Rogerian client-centered therapy and Sullivan's interpersonal psychotherapy have also shared in this resurgence of professional interest in counseling psychology and all signs indicate that they will continue to do so.

BIBLIOGRAPHY

PRIMARY SOURCES OF HARRY STACK SULLIVAN

1953a. *Conceptions of Modern Psychiatry: The First William Alanson White Memorial   Lectures*, NY: W. W. Norton & Co.

1953b. *The Interpersonal Theory of Psychiatry*, NY: W. W. Norton & Co.

1954. *The Psychiatric Interview*, NY: W. W. Norton & Co.

1956. *Clinical Studies in Psychiatry*, NY: W. W. Norton & Co.

1962. *Schizophrenia as a Human Process*, NY: W. W. Norton & Co.

1964. *The Fusion of Psychiatry and Social Science*, NY: W. W. Norton & Co.

1972. *Personal Psychopathology*, NY: W. W. Norton & Co.

SECONDARY SOURCES

Amada, Gerald. (1985) *A Guide to Psychotherapy.* NY: Madison Books.

Feist, Jess. (1985) *Theories of Personality.* NY: Holt, Rinehart and Winston.

Hall, Calvin S. and Gardner Lindzey.   (1957). *Theories of Personality.* NY: John Wiley & Sons.

Hjelle, Larry A. and Daniel J. Ziegler.   (1976). *Personality Theories: Basic Assumptions, Research, and Applications.* NY: McGraw-Hill Book Company.

Kendler, Howard H.   (1987). *Historical Foundations of Modern Psychology.* Chicago, IL: The Dorsey Press.

Lundin, Robert W.   (1985). *Theories and Systems of Psychology.* Third Edition.   Lexington, MA: D. C. Heath and Co.

Millon, Theodore. (1983). *Theories of Personality and Psychopathology,* Third Edition.   NY: Holt, Rinehart and Winston.

Morgan, John H. (2010). *Beginning with Freud: The Classical Schools of Psychotherapy.* Lima, OH: Wyndham Hall Press.

Morgan, John H. (2009). *Beyond Divine Intervention: The Biology of Right and Wrong.* Lima, OH: Wyndham Hall Press.

Morgan, John H. (2006). *Being Human: Perspectives on Meaning and Interpretation (Essays in Religion, Culture and Personality).* South Bend, IN: Cloverdale Books.

Morgan, John H. (2005). *Naturally Good: A Behavioral History of Moral Development (From Charles Darwin to E. O. Wilson)*. South Bend, IN: Cloverdale Books.

Mullahy, Patrick. (1973). *The Beginnings of Modern American Psychiatry: The Ideas of Harry Stack Sullivan*. Boston: Houghton Mufflin Company.

Mullahy, Patrick. (1970). *Psychoanalysis and Interpersonal Psychiatry: The Contributiions of Harry Stack Sullivan*. New York: Science House.

Perry, Helen Swick. (1982). *Psychiatrist of America: The Life of Harry Stack Sullivan*. Cambridge, MA: The Belknap Press of Harvard University Press.

Zeig, Jeffrey K., Edtior. (1987).*The Evolution of Psychotherapy*. NY: Brunner/Mazel, Publishers.

CHAPTER THREE

What to Do When there is Nothing to Do:

The Psychotherapeutic Value of Meaning Therapy in the Treatment of Late Life Depression

What is now more popularly called "geriatric *ennui*" in the popular psychology papers is simply a variant on the older more established field of research known as late life depression. Whatever term the clinician wishes to employ, the disturbing fact is that it is very much on the rise in American medical practice. Psychotherapeutic treatment with the goal of cure, of course, is the standard within the healing professions but when we are dealing with late life depression where there is no hope for longevity, the agenda necessarily must shift from cure to care, from treatment with the goal of renewed healthy living to a focus upon the palliative aspects of a limited prognosis. Here, then, the clinician is faced with the challenge of existential intervention with an emphasis upon the "moment" rather than the future. Elsewhere, I have written extensively upon the notion of a "happy memory" as a therapeutic door with an existentialist agenda (Morgan, 2013; 2012b; 2012c; 1012d). Being both trained in the classical schools of psychotherapy and teaching those schools for nearly fifty years at, among other places, Oxford University, has left me with a tome of clinical case studies but few effective modalities of treatment upon which to regularly rely, leaving me and the clinicians with which I work left with guessing at treatment choices and "practicing" therapy with fingers crossed. I am here and now happy to report that a treatment modality called geriatric logotherapy has come to the fore and with impressive results.

Logotherapy is a type of psychotherapeutic analysis and treatment which focuses on a *will to meaning*. It is founded upon the belief that striving to find meaning in one's life is the primary, most powerful motivating and driving force within the human experience. Sometimes called existential analysis (Frankl, 1967; 2004), logotherapy is the Third Viennese School of Psychotherapy founded by Viktor Frankl, the first and second schools were founded by Freud, called psychoanalysis, and Adler, called individual psychology (Frankl, 1963; 1969; 1997; 2001). In recent years, Victor E. Frankl has emerged as the leading proponent in psychotherapeutic circles of the centrality of the experience of "meaning" in mental health (Frankl, 1962a). Pastoral Logotherapy is the application of logotherapeutic analysis and treatment within the context of a spiritual understanding of the human situation and its relevance to mental health. Though not specifically faith-based, pastoral logotherapy is practiced within the context of a spiritual awareness of self-transcendent reality (Graber,

2004). Geriatric Logotherapy, then, is a sub-set of this analytical approach designed to address issues uniquely confronted in the pastoral encounter with the elderly.

According to Frankl, life has meaning under all circumstances, even in the direst situations. "What matters is not the meaning of life in general," Frankl suggested "but rather the specific meaning of a person's life at a given moment." Meaning is not "invented" but rather "detected," he points out. We can discover meaning in life in three different ways: (1) by doing a deed; (2) by experiencing a value -- nature, a work of art, another person, love, etc., and (3) by suffering. Frankl discounts the effective utility of the Second Viennese School of Psychotherapy, i.e., Alfred Adler and his notion of humankind's "will-to-power," by arguing that personal power in the face of suffering and in the absence of personal meaning has no visible function within the personality (Frankl, 1962b).

A concept of humanity is held, consciously or not, by every school of psychotherapy (Morgan, 2012a). We see it in Freud, Adler, and Jung, and so likewise with Frankl. That concept of the human person, suggests Frankl, affects everything, all conceptual development, all theories of treatment, all clinical perceptions. Resulting from his wartime concentration camp experience, Frankl became convinced of the *sui generus* nature of the will-to-meaning, what he later developed as logotherapy (Frankl, 1958). We must elevate this concept of the person for critical analysis from the logotherapeutic perspective if we ever hope to understand the differences in psychotherapeutic modalities of treatment. "For," explains Frankl, "a psychotherapist's concept of man ... can reinforce the patient's neurosis and, therefore, can be wholly nihilistic." For Frankl, there are three fundamental characteristics of human existence which converge to define the human person, namely, spirituality, freedom, and responsibility. This tripartite foundation inevitably affects every attempt to understand who we are and what we are to do. Frankl labored hard and long for a philosophical structure to logotherapy, believing that any model of psychotherapeutic analysis and treatment must have a strong philosophical basis (Frankl, 1961b).

Neither a proponent nor an opponent of a faith-based worldview *per se*, Frankl simply intends for spirituality not to be tied up with a specific notion of religion. Where faith helps a person through the day, Frankl has no objection to it. Where religious worldview and ethos stifle, cripple, or delude an individual, Frankl is opposed to it. What Frankl means by "spirituality" as a fundamental component of human nature is man's capacity for a sense of awe, wonder, and mystery, even reverence, in one's assessing the meaning, value, and purpose of one's own personal life. The surprising feature about Frankl's psychotherapeutic formulations is that throughout he consistently makes inferential comments about the religious dynamic operative in his own theory while constantly omitting any specific reference to its fundamentally Jewish character (Frankl, 1957; 1961a). The connectedness of all things as experienced in moments of high sensitivity or even ecstasy is the role spirituality plays in the human character. A deeply felt sense of beauty, power, and wonder in the universe, a heightened experience of integrality, what I have in another place chosen to call "systemic integrality," constitutes what spirituality means in logotherapy (Morgan, 2009). "By helping prisoners then and patients later remember their past lives – their joys, sorrows, sacrifices, and blessings – he emphasized the "meaningfulness" of their lives as already lived (Frankl,1954)." Whether one is a theist, an atheist, or an agnostic, Frankl contends that the dynamics of spirituality can be equally and meaningfully operate within a person's life bringing value and purpose.

Complimenting this sense of spirituality within the logotherapeutic model is a freedom which functions in the face of three things: (1) the instincts; (2) inherited disposition; and (3) environment. Frankl engages in a long and definitive discussion of freedom in his celebrated classic, *The Doctor and the Soul*, owing no doubt to his own personal encounter with the existential vacuum during his trying experiences in captivity. The converging of these three components of instincts, heredity, and environment constitutes the matrix out of which the human experience of freedom can grow and thrive in a person's life. To rise above one's instincts, says Frankl, is a distinctively human possibility and, unlike Freud's obsession with the power of instincts governing human behavior, Frankl specifically calls upon the responsible person to take his instincts in hand, use them but control them, for service to others. Likewise with heritage, one cannot deny one's own genetic composition but in the acknowledging of it one asserts power over its domination. A determinist, Frankl was most certainly not. He believed in the human person's ability to respond responsibly to self-knowledge. He emphasizes not only the recollected past, but calls attention to the existential meaningfulness of suffering and tragedy in life as testimonies to human courage and dignity (Frankl, 1961c). By knowing one's instincts and one's genetic heritage comes a source of strength and power to control, direct, and utilize the primordial nature of these characteristics for the good of self and humanity.

Finally, Frankl was not a member of the "nurture" crowd of behavioral psychologists who would attribute, even blame, one's social and physical environment for the way individuals turn out in their maturity. These three fundamental components of freedom, namely, instincts, heritage, and environment, may be used by the human person to realize freedom if he becomes aware of them, embraces them, and directs them towards a meaningful purpose in life. In logotherapy, Frankl differentiates meaning and values. Values are socially held meanings whereas "meaning as the *sine qua non* of life is a unique experience and possession of every single individual in every moment of one's own life (Frankl, 1961d)."

Besides spirituality and freedom, however, there is responsibility. Having been greatly influenced in his formative years with the writings of the existentialists, not least being Kierkegaard, Sartre, and Heidegger, Frankl was most insistent that in order for a person to be fully human, he must exercise responsibility. The individual is responsible to his own conscience first and foremost, says Frankl. Conscience, he suggests, is a "thing in itself," it is *sui generis*. It is so fundamental to the human person that humanity cannot exist without it nor the human person remain human without it. Conscience has to do with the drive to do the right thing because it is the right thing to do. This is so fundamental to the human experience that without it neither humanity nor civilization itself could exist. Of course, the "origin" of conscience is a point of controversy and contention within the various schools of psychotherapy and depth psychology. The three schools of thought regarding the origins of ethics and moral behavior I have discussed at length elsewhere, first in my book *Naturally Good: A Behavioral History of Moral Development* (2005), and more specifically the three school as Ethical Theism, Ethical Humanism, and Ethical Naturalism in my book *Beyond Divine Intervention: The Biology of Right and Wrong* (2009).

More so with Frankl than with any other psychotherapist, the personal life story of each individual proved to be a major factor in the development of his own therapeutic system of theory and practice. Frankl contended that this will-to-meaning – as Freud argued for "pleasure" and Adler for "power" – pervades every secret recess of one's personal life. Meaning, he pointed out, can be found in any situation within which we find ourselves (Frankl, 1953). Freud's life, Adler's life, and Jung's life have all proven interesting and have in their own way shown how their life and work were integrated. But with Frankl, it is inconceivable to imagine logotherapy as a school of thought being produced in the absence of his concentration camp experience. The viability of his theory and the utility of his clinical practice both rely upon the life history of its creator. Frankl's relevance to contemporary treatment in therapeutic settings is becoming increasingly recognized and appreciated within a broad spectrum of clinical practice. The impact of his therapeutic system of theory and treatment has yet to reach its maximum level of influence in contemporary counseling circles but the establishment of the Graduate Center for Pastoral Logotherapy at the Graduate Theological Foundation under the direction of Dr. Ann Graber (Graber, 2004) constitutes a major leap forward in this development.

When logotherapy is applied to the geriatric patient, there is a challenge to transform the central concepts of the therapeutic practice to the life situation of the individual whose life has, for all practical purpose, already been lived. Believing that logotherapy has, indeed, something yet to offer the geriatric patient, it is imperative that the "will to meaning" not be only thought of as an agenda for future living but as a hermeneutic for "living in the moment." Existential episodes of happiness constitute what the clinician might imagine to be the practical application of logotherapy in dealing with older and elderly individuals (Morgan, 2006a; 2006b). Rather than seeking for that window of hope for the future which is so characteristic of this modality of therapeutic practice, the logotherapist must creatively search for "existential episodes of happiness," as I have chosen to call them, viz., remembered events in which the older person demonstrably attributes the experience of "happiness."

The interpretive hermeneutic of pastoral logotherapy, rather than focusing upon hope for a cure of the depression and ennui being experienced by the late life patient, focuses rather upon memories, times past which bring a moment of reflective happiness now. The intent is to explication from an existential memory of happy recollection a deeper sense of the meaningfulness of life as lived in the moment. Meaningful, in this therapeutic instance, constitutes a matrix of converging memory and existential happiness and provides a practical formula for therapeutic application when dealing with both terminal patients so diagnosed as well as late life depression patients whose cognitive functions offer a broader range of access to recollected memories. The existential character of the remembered happy event constitutes the possibility for a treasure trove of episodic happiness vignettes bringing comfort to the elderly facing a limited future.

Illustrative of this existential moment or window of happiness is the case of Mrs. Williams, a nursing home patient in her mid-80s suffering from acute and depression. Other complicating health issues included high blood pressure, diabetes, and arthritis. A retired librarian for some twenty-plus years, Mrs. Williams came to the nursing home after falling in her home where she lived alone. The decision was made for institutional care in conjunction with family members (all distant cousins as she was widowed with no children). In meeting with her over several sessions, the therapist struggled with finding the "door of happy memories" through which to follow Mrs. Williams.

Finally, during the third clinical session, some passing reference was made to her childhood farm life and swimming with her girlfriends in the cow pond behind the barn. As this passing reference seemed to cause her to pause and smile as she was formulaically reciting her "life's story" to the therapist, it became clear to the observing therapist that she enjoyed the memory and might enjoy elaborating upon it. The result was a meandering recollection of her childhood experiences with her friends on the family farm which, she said, "I haven't thought of in years." Subsequent sessions always harped back to these happy memories and provided a substance to her solitary reflections beyond the therapy sessions.

Often, the geriatric patient needs assistance in conjuring these past episodes of happiness and the therapist then can employ what I have chosen to call "memory suggestions," viz., asking the individual to back track consciously in search of "illustrative events" in his or her life to which they themselves attribute a blissful and happy experience. However, an important key here for the therapist to keep in mind is "stress avoidance," that is, redirecting the individual away from remembered events in their past which clearly, by facial expression or voice intonation, suggest stress or anxiety or unhappiness (Morgan, 2010). Family history is quite frequently the source of these happiness episodes but the therapist is advised to watch carefully lest the family history stories drift downward into negative memories.

It is crucial that the therapist keep in mind the logotherapeutic agenda lest one imagine that the purpose and goal of the therapeutic session is to search out the "meaning and purpose of life" yet to be lived. With the older and elderly patient, the acutely practical nature of the existential utility and viability of therapy must always be kept in the forefront of the therapeutic encounter when employing logotherapeutic analysis. Though sometimes a challenge in dealing with the elderly (geriatric dementia often manifests itself in the individual's disinclination to converse), the therapist must employ what I have chosen to call "points of conversation" as an impetus and incentive for the geriatric patient to engage the therapist in the quest for existential episodes of happiness (Morgan, 1987). Places, times, and people constitute for me the three fundamental arenas within which the patient may find these points of conversation leading to the "discovery" and "revisiting" of happiness episodes in their earlier life.

Another example of geriatric logotherapy is the case of Dr. Watson, a retired philosophy professor living alone in his home as a widower with two adult children living far away. Dr. Watson is in his late 80s, was once a nationally recognized scholar, author of several books, but these days finds reading increasingly difficult owing to glaucoma and writing virtually impossible due to arthritis in both hands. Reduced to sitting on his expansive front porch when weather permits and before the fireplace otherwise, Dr. Watson has sunk into a debilitating depression resulting in a consistent failure to eat regularly or to converse over the phone with friends and family. A concerned son precipitated the contact with a logotherapist who made an initial home visit, finding the above situation. Dr. Watson had essentially "given up," as he put it, because of an inability to read or write, his life's work and passion. When the therapist encouraged the professor to "tell me about your life's work," Dr. Watson commenced slowly and deliberately rattling off his educational background, teaching appointments, books written, conferences attended, all with little passion and near expressionless. However, when the therapist asked about specific colleagues mentioned in the monotone narrative, he noticed that the patient became somewhat animated, enthusiastic, even excited to relate story after story involving colleagues, happy stories, fun stories, all leading to an extremely productive journey through time and people of importance. Subsequent sessions centered upon the same topics with the results that Dr. Watson began calling old friends, inviting other retired colleagues in town to come for morning coffee and chat. The door of happy memories had been opened and entered and Dr. Watson's life took on renewed vitality.

One of the greatest challenges for the logotherapist is to acknowledge and own the inevitable reality of the brevity of life left to the elderly patient. The therapeutic goal here is clearly not some form of contrived "cure" for what might be the presenting symptoms of depression which is most commonly the driving force in seeking help for the patient either by the patient or the family or residential institutional staff responsible for caring for the patient. A cure certainly is not what is sought here, but rather, beyond and after the notion of a cure for the aged patient, there is an urgent need for the identification of the "rightful place for palliative care" in such situations. A quest for existential happiness, episodic joy from happy memories, constitutes the driving force in the therapeutic encounter with the geriatric patient who most commonly is suffering from depression.

A concluding illustration of the value of geriatric logotherapy and its use in existential counseling is the case of Miss Horton, an elderly unmarried school teacher from a small town, whose life had been synonymous with teaching elementary school children, living in the background, watching them grow up, move away, establish families, and launch careers. Now nearly 90 years old residing in an assisted living facility in her little town, she had drifted into depression owing to a lack of social stimulus (most other residents were suffering from acute and severely debilitating geriatric dementia). Her health had declined gradually owing to heart problems and towards the end of her life, she had taken to the bed and less and less willing to converse with even the nurses. The nursing director called in the logotherapist (based on the therapist's reputation in dealing with geriatric dementia) and from the beginning the initial encounter was fruitless, bordering on hopeless. As the therapist explored Miss Horton's social life through interviews with nursing staff who knew the patient's personal history and in the therapist's search for the "magic door" that would introduce happy memories and reflective thoughts of joys gone by, it occurred to him that since her life had been lived for the children she taught, why not get some of those children, now adults, to come say goodbye to her in her closing days of life. It worked wonders. Through the local school, the therapist was able to contact several of her past students, now parents and successful people, to come for a visit. Since most people are uncomfortable visiting someone on their death bed, the therapist always arranged to be present, coaching the visitor to help Miss Horton "remember" episodes in the classroom and on the playground in which she was a major player and to share with her, as she lay mute but alert, the stories of their own lives as they left school and entered the world, always with reference to her contribution to their own personal lives. The results were remarkable, not that she lived much longer, for she did not, but during the closing weeks of her life, she became conversant, sitting up in bed, asking about this student and that student, remembering to the therapist more and more "happy moments" in her teaching life that brought a twinkle to her eyes and a smile on her face.

Unlike other schools of thought which too frequently presume to be the panacea for all mental disorders, logotherapy has self-consciously identified its arenas of success and knows those in which it has little or no value.

The distinctions center around psychogenic and biogenic classifications. Certainly and with little contradiction, logotherapy has a long clinical history of effective use in the treatment of psychogenic depression. When applied to the treatment of the elderly, not as a curative but as a palliative therapy, there is a promise of great success. The encroachment of *ennui* upon the elderly, particularly and especially those who have been actively engaged in a full life of service such as the clergy, physicians, teachers, and attorneys, can be a traumatic and debilitating experience. To come to the end of a productive and meaningful life of service with an existential sense of nothing to do and nothing left to do but drift off into geriatric dementia, the patient finds it difficult to cry out for help, not knowing or realizing what actually is happening to him or her. When it is not hope for the future which is being sought but rather an effective and celebrative address to the existential realities confronting the elderly patient who is facing decline and death, the quest for those "happy moments" conjured in the patient's memory constitute a promising field of treatment. Geriatric logotherapy is uniquely constructed to do just that.

END NOTES:

(1953) Frankl, Viktor. "Logos and Existence in Psychotherapy," *American Journal of Psychotherapy,* VII: 8-15.

(1954) Frankl, Viktor. "Group Psychotherapeutic Experiences in a Concentration Camp," *Group Psychotherapy*, VII: 81-90.

(1957) Frankl, Viktor. "The Spiritual Dimension in Existential Analysis and Logotherapy," *Journal of Individual Psychology*, XV: 157-165.

(1958) Frankl, Viktor. "The Will to Meaning," *The Journal of Pastoral Care,* XII: 82-88.

(1961a) Frankl, Viktor. "Religion and Existential Psychotherapy," *The Gordon Review,* VI: 2-10.

(1961b) Frank, Viktor. "Psychotherapy and Philosophy," *Philosophy Today,* v: 59-64.

(1961c) Frankl, Viktor. "Logotherapy and the Challenge of Suffering," *Review of Existential Psychology and Psychiatry,* I: 3-7.

(1961d) Frankl, Viktor. "Dynamics, Existence and Values," *Journal of Existential Psychiatry,* II: 5-16.

(1962a) Frankl, Viktor. "Psychiatry and Man's Quest for Meaning," *Journal of Religion and Health,* I:93-103.

(1962b) Frankl, Viktor. "Logotherapy and the Challenge of Suffering," *Pastoral Psychology,* XIII:25-28.

(1963) Frankl, Viktor. *Man's Search for Meaning. An Introduction to Logotherapy.* Boston: Beacon Press.

(1967) Frank, Viktor. *Psychotherapy and Existentialism: Selected Papers on Logotherapy.* New York: Simon & Schuster.

(1969) Frankl, Viktor. *The Will to Meaning: Foundations and Applications of Logotherapy.* New York: New American Library.

(1997) Frankl, Viktor. *Man's Search for Ultimate Meaning.* New York: Basic Books

(2001) Frankl, Viktor. *Man's Search for Ultimate Meaning: A Psychology Exploration of the Religious Quest.* (With a Foreword by Swanee Hunt). MJF Books.

(2004) Frankl, Viktor. *On the Theory and Therapy of Mental Disorders: An Introduction to Logotherapy and Existential Analysis.* (James M. DuBois, Trans.). London: Routledge.

(2004) Graber, Ann V. *Viktor Frankl's Logotherapy: Method of Choice in Ecumenical Pastoral Psychology* (2nd ed.). Lima, OH: Wyndham Hall Press.

(1987) Morgan, John H. *From Freud to Frankl: Our Modern Search for Personal Meaning.* Bristol, IN: Wyndham Hall Press.

(2005) Morgan, John H. *Naturally Good: A Behavioral History of Moral Development* (South Bend, IN: Cloverdale Books).

(2006a) Morgan, John H. *Being Human: Perspectives on Meaning and Interpretation (Essays in Religion, Culture and Personality)* (2nd ed.). South Bend, IN: Cloverdale Books.

(2006b) "Personal Meaning as Psychotherapy: The Interpretive Hermeneutic of Viktor Frankl,"
in *FOUNDATION THEOLOGY,* Chapter 5 (South Bend, IN: GTF Books).

(2009) Morgan, John H. *Beyond Divine Intervention: The Biology of Right and Wrong.* Lima, OH: Wyndham Hall Press.

(2010) Morgan, John H. *Clinical Pastoral Psychotherapy: A Practitioner's Handbook for Ministry Professionals.* Mishawaka, IN: Graduate Theological Foundation.

(2012a) Morgan, John H. *Beginning With Freud: The Classical Schools of Psychotherapy* (Expanded 2nd Edition). Lima, OH: Wyndham Hall Press.

(2012b) Morgan, John H. "Geriatric Logotherapy: Exploring the Psychotherapeutics of Memory in Treating the Elderly," *Psychological Thought, Vol. 5, #2,* 2012:99-105.

(2012c) Morgan, John H. "Pastoral Nurture of the Elderly: The 'Happy Memory' in Geriatric Logotherapy"in *CLINICAL PASTORAL PSYCHOTHERAPY: A Practitioner's Handbook for Ministry Professionals* Expanded 2nd Edition (Mishawaka, IN: GTF Books, 2012).

(2012d) Morgan, John H. "Medication and Counseling in Psychiatric Practice: Biogenic Psychopharmacology and Psychogenic Psychotherapy (Partnering in the Treatment of Mental Illness)," in *CLINICAL PASTORAL PSYCHOTHERAPY: A Practitioner's Handbook for Ministry Professionals* Expanded 2nd Edition (Mishawaka, IN: GTF Books, 2012).

(2013) Morgan, John H. "Late-Life Depression and the Counseling Agenda: Exploring Geriatric Logotherapy as aTreatment Modality," *International Journal of Psychological Research* 6(1), 2013, pp. 8-15.

CHAPTER FOUR
Late-Life Depression and the Counseling Agenda:
Exploring Geriatric Logotherapy as a Treatment Modality

Geriatric Logotherapy constitutes an application of the psychotherapeutic method of treatment developed by Viktor Frankl but adapted to the care and treatment of the elderly. Logotherapy is a type of psychotherapeutic analysis and treatment which focuses on a *will to meaning*. It is founded upon the belief that striving to find meaning in one's life is the primary, most powerful motivating and driving force within the human experience. Sometimes called existential analysis (Frankl, 1967; 2004), logotherapy is the Third Viennese School of Psychotherapy founded by Viktor Frankl, the first and second schools were founded by Freud, called psychoanalysis, and Adler, called individual psychology (Frankl, 1963; 1969; 1997; 2001). In recent years, it has emerged as a leading school of thought emphasizing the psychotherapeutic centrality of the experience of "meaning" in mental health (Frankl, 1962a). Pastoral Logotherapy is the application of logotherapeutic analysis and treatment within the context of a spiritual understanding of the human situation and its relevance to mental health. Though not specifically faith-based, pastoral logotherapy is practiced within the context of a spiritual awareness of self-transcendent reality (Graber, 2004). Geriatric Logotherapy, then, is a sub-set of this analytical approach designed to address issues uniquely confronted in the therapeutic counseling of the elderly.

According to logotherapeutic analysis, life has meaning under all circumstances, even in the direst situations. "What matters is not the meaning of life in general," logotherapists suggest, "but rather the specific meaning of a person's life at a given moment." Meaning is not "invented" but rather "detected," he points out. We can discover meaning in life in three different ways: (1) by doing a deed; (2) by experience a value -- nature, a work of art, another person, love, etc., and (3) by suffering. Discounting the effective utility of the Second Viennese School of Psychotherapy, i.e., Alfred Adler and his notion of the "will-to-power," logotherapists would have us understand that merely personal power, in the face of suffering and in the absence of personal meaning, has no viable function within the personality itself (Frankl, 1962b).

A concept of humanity is held, consciously or not, by every school of psychotherapy (Morgan, 2012). We see it in Freud's psychoanalysis, Adler's individual psychology, and Jung's analaytical psychology, and so likewise with Frankl's logotherapy. Whatever that concept of the human person might be, it affects everything, all conceptual development, all theories of treatment, all clinical perceptions. Resulting from his wartime concentration camp experience, Frankl became convinced of the *sui generus* nature of the will-to-meaning, what he later developed as logotherapy (Frankl, 1958). We must elevate this concept of the person for critical analysis from the logotherapeutic perspective if we ever hope to understand the differences in psychotherapeutic modalities of treatment. "For," it should be pointed out, "a psychotherapist's concept of man … can reinforce the patient's neurosis and, therefore, can be wholly nihilistic." In logotherapy theory, there are three fundamental characteristics of human existence which converge to define the human person, namely, spirituality, freedom, and responsibility. This tripartite foundation inevitably affects every attempt to understand who we are and what we are to do. Laboring hard and long for a philosophical structure to logotherapy, clinical practitioners believe that any model of psychotherapeutic analysis and treatment must have a strong philosophical basis (Frankl, 1961b).

Neither a proponent nor an opponent of a faith-based worldview *per se*, logotherapy simply intends for spirituality not to be tied up with a specific notion of religion.   Where faith helps a person through the day, logotherapists have no objection to it.   Where religious worldview and ethos stifle, cripple, or delude an individual, logotherapy as a psychotherapeutic modality of treatment is very much opposed to it.   What Frankl means by "spirituality" as a fundamental component of human nature is man's capacity for a sense of awe, wonder, and mystery, even reverence, in one's assessing the meaning, value, and purpose of one's own personal life. The surprising feature about this psychotherapeutic formulation is the fact that logotherapists consistently make inferential comments about the religious dynamic operative in its theoretical development while constantly omitting any specific reference to its fundamentally religious character (Frankl, 1957; 1961a).   The connectedness of all things as experienced in moments of high sensitivity or even ecstasy is the role spirituality plays in the human character.   A deeply felt sense of beauty, power, and wonder in the universe, a heightened experience of integrality, what I have in another place chosen to call "systemic integrality," constitutes what spirituality means in logotherapy (Morgan, 2009).   "By helping prisoners then and patients later remember their past lives – their joys, sorrows, sacrifices, and blessings – Frankl emphasized the "meaningfulness" of their lives as already lived (Frankl,1954)." Whether one is a theist, an atheist, or an agnostic, logotherapists contend that the dynamics of spirituality can be equally and meaningfully operate within a person's life bringing value and purpose.

Complimenting this sense of spirituality within the logotherapeutic model is a freedom which functions in the face of three things: (1) the instincts; (2) inherited disposition; and (3) environment. The converging of these three components of instincts, heredity, and environment constitutes the matrix out of which the human experience of freedom can grow and thrive in a person's life. The ability to rise above one's instincts, certainly, is a distinctively human possibility and, unlike Freud's obsession with the power of instincts governing human behavior, logotheray specifically calls upon the responsible person to take one's instincts in hand, use them but control them, for service to others. Likewise with heritage, one cannot deny one's own genetic composition but in the acknowledging of it one asserts power over its domination. Logotherapists have confidence in the human person's ability to respond responsibly to self-knowledge. Practitioners of logotherapy emphasize not only the recollected past, but call attention to the existential meaningfulness of suffering and tragedy in life as living testimonials to human courage and dignity (Frankl, 1961c). By knowing one's instincts and one's genetic heritage comes a source of strength and power to control, direct, and utilize the primordial nature of these characteristics for the good of self and humanity.

Avoiding the reductionistic pitfalls of behaviorism which is inclined to blame one's social and physical environment for the causes of personality dysfunction, logotherapy calls rather for an assertion of the primacy of individual responsibility in the face of life's presenting situational constraints upon personality development. These three fundamental components of freedom, namely, instincts, heritage, and environment, may be used by the human person to realize freedom if he becomes aware of them, embraces them, and directs them towards a meaningful purpose in life. In logotherapy, there is a self-conscious differentiation between meaning and values. Values are socially held meanings whereas "meaning as the *sine qua non* of life is a unique experience and possession of every single individual in every moment of one's own life (Frankl, 1961d)."

Besides spirituality and freedom, however, there is responsibility. Having been greatly influenced in its developmental years with the writings of the existentialists, especially Kierkegaard, Sartre, and Heidegger, logotherapists are insistent that in order for a person to be fully human, the individual must exercise responsibility. The individual is responsible to his own conscience first and foremost. Conscience is a "thing in itself," it is *sui generis*. It is so fundamental to the human person that humanity cannot exist without it nor the human person remain human without it. Conscience has to do with the drive to do the right thing because it is the right thing to do. This is so fundamental to the human experience that without it neither humanity nor civilization itself could exist. Of course, the "origin" of conscience is a point of controversy and contention within the various schools of psychotherapy and depth psychology. The three schools of thought regarding the origins of ethics and moral behavior I have discussed at length elsewhere, first in my book *Naturally Good: A Behavioral History of Moral Development* (2005), and more specifically the three school as Ethical Theism, Ethical Humanism, and Ethical Naturalism in my book *Beyond Divine Intervention: The Biology of Right and Wrong* (2009).

More so with logotherapy than with other psychotherapies, the personal life story of each individual proves to be a major factor in the development of any therapeutic system of theory and practice. Frankl contended that this "will-to-meaning" – as Freud argued for "pleasure" and Adler for "power" – pervades every secret recess of one's personal life. Meaning, we must point out, can be found in any situation within which we find ourselves (Frankl, 1953). Freud's life, Adler's life, and Jung's life have all proven interesting and have in their own way shown how their life and work were integrated. The viability of any theory and the utility of its clinical practice both rely upon the life history of its creator. For example, Frankl's relevance to contemporary treatment in therapeutic settings is becoming increasingly recognized and appreciated within a broad spectrum of clinical practice. The impact of his therapeutic system of theory and treatment has yet to reach its maximum level of influence in contemporary counseling circles but the establishment of the Graduate Center for Pastoral Logotherapy at the Graduate Theological Foundation under the direction of Dr. Ann Graber (Graber, 2004) constitutes a major leap forward in this development.

When logotherapy is applied to the geriatric patient, there is a challenge to transform the central concepts of the therapeutic practice to the life situation of the individual whose life has, for all practical purpose, already been lived. Believing that logotherapy has, indeed, something yet to offer the geriatric patient, it is imperative that the "will to meaning" not be only thought of as an agenda for future living but as a hermeneutic for "living in the moment." Existential episodes of happiness constitute what the clinician might imagine to be the practical application of logotherapy in dealing with older and elderly individuals (Morgan, 2006). Rather than seeking for that window of hope for the future which is so characteristic of this modality of therapeutic practice, the logotherapist must creatively search for "existential episodes of happiness," as I have chosen to call them, viz., remembered events in which the older person demonstrably attributes the experience of "happiness." This approach, rather than focusing upon hope, focuses upon memories, times past which bring a moment of reflective happiness now. The existential character of the remembered happy event constitutes the possibility for a treasure trove of episodic happiness vignettes bringing comfort to the elderly facing a limited future.

Illustrative of this existential moment or window of happiness is the case of Mrs. Williams, a nursing home patient in her mid-80s suffering from acute and near debilitating depression. Other complicating health issues included high blood pressure, diabetes, and arthritis. A retired librarian for some twenty-plus years, Mrs. Williams came to the nursing home after falling in her home where she lived alone. The decision was made for institutional care in conjunction with family members (all distant cousins as she was widowed with no children). In meeting with her over several sessions, the therapist struggled with finding the "door of happy memories" through which to follow Mrs. Williams. Finally, during the third clinical session, some passing reference was made to her childhood farm life and swimming with her girlfriends in the cow pond behind the barn. As this passing reference seemed to cause her to pause and smile as she was formulaically reciting her "life's story" to the therapist, it became clear to the observing therapist that she enjoyed the memory and might enjoy elaborating upon it. The result was a meandering recollection of her childhood experiences with her friends on the family farm which, she said, "I haven't thought of in years." Subsequent sessions always harped back to these happy memories and provided a substance to her solitary reflections beyond the therapy sessions.

Often, the geriatric patient needs assistance in conjuring these past episodes of happiness and the therapist then can employ what I have chosen to call "memory suggestions," viz., asking the individual to back track consciously in search of "illustrative events" in his or her life to which they themselves attribute a blissful and happy experience. However, an important key here for the therapist to keep in mind is "stress avoidance," that is, redirecting the individual away from remembered events in their past which clearly, by facial expression or voice intonation, suggest stress or anxiety or unhappiness (Morgan, 2010). Family history is quite frequently the source of these happiness episodes but the therapist is advised to watch carefully lest the family history stories drift downward into negative memories.

It is crucial that the therapist keep in mind the logotherapeutic agenda lest one imagine that the purpose and goal of the therapeutic session is to search out the "meaning and purpose of life" yet to be lived. With the older and elderly patient, the acutely practical nature of the existential utility and viability of therapy must always be kept in the forefront of the therapeutic encounter when employing logotherapeutic analysis. Though sometimes a challenge in dealing with the elderly (geriatric dementia often manifests itself in the individual's disinclination to converse), the therapist must employ what I have chosen to call "points of conversation" as an impetus and incentive for the geriatric patient to engage the therapist in the quest for existential episodes of happiness (Morgan, 1987). Places, times, and people constitute for me the three fundamental arenas within which the patient may find these points of conversation leading to the "discovery" and "revisiting" of happiness episodes in their earlier life.

Another example of geriatric logotherapy is the case of Dr. Watson, a retired philosophy professor living alone in his home as a widower with two adult children living far away. Dr. Watson is in his late 80s, was once a nationally recognized scholar, author of several books, but these days finds reading increasingly difficult owing to glaucoma and writing virtually impossible due to arthritis in both hands. Reduced to sitting on his expansive front porch when weather permits and before the fireplace otherwise, Dr. Watson has sunk into a debilitating depression resulting in a consistent failure to eat regularly or to converse over the phone with friends and family. A concerned son precipitated the contact with a logotherapist who made an initial home visit, finding the above situation. Dr. Watson had essentially "given up," as he put it, because of an inability to read or write, his life's work and passion. When the therapist encouraged the professor to "tell me about your life's work," Dr. Watson commenced slowly and deliberately rattling off his educational background, teaching appointments, books written, conferences attended, all with little passion and near expressionless. However, when the therapist asked about specific colleagues mentioned in the monotone narrative, he noticed that the patient became somewhat animated, enthusiastic, even excited to relate story after story involving colleagues, happy stories, fun stories, all leading to an extremely productive journey through time and people of importance. Subsequent sessions centered upon the same topics with the results that Dr. Watson began calling old friends, inviting other retired colleagues in town to come for morning coffee and chat. The door of happy memories had been opened and entered and Dr. Watson's life took on renewed vitality.

One of the greatest challenges for the logotherapist is to acknowledge and own the inevitable reality of the brevity of life left to the elderly patient. The therapeutic goal here is clearly not some form of contrived "cure" for what might be the presenting symptoms of depression which is most commonly the driving force in seeking help for the patient either by the patient or the family or residential institutional staff responsible for caring for the patient. A cure certainly is not what is sought here, but rather, beyond and after the notion of a cure for the aged patient, there is an urgent need for the identification of the "rightful place for palliative care" in such situations. A quest for existential happiness, episodic joy from happy memories, constitutes the driving force in the therapeutic encounter with the geriatric patient who most commonly is suffering from depression.

A concluding illustration of the value of geriatric logotherapy and its use in existential counseling is the case of Miss Horton, an elderly spinster school teacher from a small town, whose life had been synonymous with teaching elementary school children, living in the background, watching them grow up, move away, establish families, and launch careers. Now nearly 90 years old residing in an assisted living facility in her little town, she had drifted into depression owing to a lack of social stimulus (most other residents were suffering from acute and severely debilitating geriatric dementia). Her health had declined gradually owing to heart problems and towards the end of her life, she had taken to the bed and less and less willing to converse with even the nurses. The nursing director called in the logotherapist (based on the therapist's reputation in dealing with geriatric dementia) and from the beginning the initial encounter was fruitless, boarding only hopeless. As the therapist explored Miss Horton's social life through interviews with nursing staff who knew the patient's personal history and in the therapist's search for the "magic door" that would introduce happy memories and reflective thoughts of joys gone by, it occurred to him that since her life had been lived for the children she taught, why not get some of those children, now adults, to come say goodbye to her in her closing days of life. It worked wonders. Through the local school, the therapist was able to contact several of her past students, now parents and successful people, to come for a visit. Since most people are uncomfortable visiting someone on their death bed, the therapist always arranged to be present, coaching the visitor to help Miss Horton "remember" episodes in the classroom and on the playground in which she was a major player and to share with her, as she lay mute but alert, the stories of their own lives as they left school and entered the world, always with reference to her contribution to their own personal lives. The results were remarkable, not that she lived much longer, for she did not, but during the closing weeks of her life, she became conversant, sitting up in bed, asking about this student and that student, remembering to the therapist more and more "happy moments" in her teaching life that brought a twinkle to her eyes and a smile on her face.

The therapeutic limits of logotherapy, never claimed to be a comprehensive analytical modality for all types of mental illness, are readily acknowledged. Unlike other schools of thought, which too frequently presume to be the panacea for all mental disorders, logotherapy has self-consciously identified its arenas of success and knows those in which it has little or no value. The distinctions it makes in its value and utility center around the clinical and practical differences between psychogenic and biogenic classifications. Certainly and with little contradiction, logotherapy has a long clinical history of effective use in the treatment of psychogenic depression. When applied to the treatment of the elderly, not as a curative but as a palliative therapy, there is a promise of great success as well. For those in clinical practice, the growing instances of reported success in the use of geriatric logotherapy constitute a cause for a more systematic assessment of case studies in such applications. Empirical demonstration of the effectiveness of this modality of treatment is on the rise within long-term health care facilities for the elderly and the medical and psychotherapeutic community is well poised to evaluate and implement methods which show signs of value and utility. When hope for curative therapy is not that which is being sought by the psychotherapist but rather an effective and celebrative address to the existential realities confronting the elderly patient facing decline and death, the quest for those "happy moments" conjured in the patient's memory constitute a promising field of treatment. Geriatric logotherapy is uniquely constituted to do just that.

END NOTES:

(1953) "Logos and Existence in Psychotherapy," *American Journal of Psychotherapy,* VII: 8-15.

(1954) "Group Psychotherapeutic Experiences in a Concentration Camp," *Group Psychotherapy,* VII: 81-90.

(1957) "The Spiritual Dimension in Existential Analysis and Logotherapy," *Journal of Individual Psychology,* XV: 157-165.

(1958) "The Will to Meaning," *The Journal of Pastoral Care,* XII: 82-88.

(1961a) "Religion and Existential Psychotherapy," *The Gordon Review,* VI: 2-10.

(1961b) "Psychotherapy and Philosophy," *Philosophy Today,* v: 59-64.

(1961c) "Logotherapy and the Challenge of Suffering," *Review of Existential Psychology and Psychiatry,* I: 3-7.

(1961d) "Dynamics, Existence and Values," *Journal of Existential Psychiatry,* II: 5-16.

(1962a) "Psychiatry and Man's Quest for Meaning," *Journal of Religion and Health,* I:93-103.

(1962b) "Logotherapy and the Challenge of Suffering," *Pastoral Psychology,* XIII:25-28.

(1963). *Man's Search for Meaning. An Introduction to Logotherapy.* Boston: Beacon Press.

(1967). *Psychotherapy and Existentialism: Selected Papers on Logotherapy.* New York: Simon & Schuster.

(1969). *The Will to Meaning: Foundations and Applications of Logotherapy.* New York: New American Library.

(1997). *Man's Search for Ultimate Meaning.* New York: Basic Books

(2001). *Man's Search for Ultimate Meaning: A Psychology Exploration of the Religious Quest.* (With a Foreword by Swanee Hunt). MJF Books.

(2004). *On the Theory and Therapy of Mental Disorders: An Introduction to Logotherapy and Existential Analysis.* (James M. DuBois, Trans.). London: Routledge.

(2004) Graber, Ann V. *Viktor Frankl's Logotherapy: Method of Choice in Ecumenical Pastoral Psychology* (2nd ed.). Lima, OH: Wyndham Hall Press.

(1987) Morgan, John H. *From Freud to Frankl: Our Modern Search for Personal Meaning.* Bristol, IN: Wyndham Hall Press.

(2005) Morgan, John H. *Naturally Good: A Behavioral History of Moral Development* (South Bend, IN: Cloverdale Books).

(2006) Morgan, John H. *Being Human: Perspectives on Meaning and Interpretation (Essays in Religion, Culture and Personality)* (2nd ed.). South Bend, IN: Cloverdale Books.

(2009) Morgan, John H. *Beyond Divine Intervention: The Biology of Right and Wrong.* Lima, OH: Wyndham Hall Press.

(2010) Morgan, John H. *Clinical Pastoral Psychotherapy: A Practitioner's Handbook for Ministry Professionals.* Mishawaka, IN: Graduate Theological Foundation.

(2012) Morgan, John H. *Beginning With Freud: The Classical Schools of Psychotherapy* (Expanded 2nd Edition). Lima, OH: Wyndham Hall Press.

CHAPTER FIVE
Geriatric Logotherapy: Exploring the Psychotherapeutics of Memory in Treating the Elderly

Logotherapy is a type of psychotherapeutic analysis and treatment which focuses on a *will to meaning*. It is founded upon the belief that striving to find meaning in one's life is the primary, most powerful motivating and driving force within the human experience. Sometimes called existential analysis (Frankl, 1967; 2004), logotherapy is the Third Viennese School of Psychotherapy founded by Viktor Frankl, the first and second schools were founded by Freud, called psychoanalysis, and Adler, called individual psychology (Frankl, 1963; 1969; 1997; 2001). In recent years, Victor E. Frankl has emerged as the leading proponent in psychotherapeutic circles of the centrality of the experience of "meaning" in mental health (Frankl, 1962a). Pastoral Logotherapy is the application of logotherapeutic analysis and treatment within the context of a spiritual understanding of the human situation and its relevance to mental health. Though not specifically faith-based, pastoral logotherapy is practiced within the context of a spiritual awareness of self-transcendent reality (Graber, 2004). Geriatric Logotherapy, then, is a sub-set of this analytical approach designed to address issues uniquely confronted in the pastoral encounter with the elderly.

According to Frankl, life has meaning under all circumstances, even in the direst situations. "What matters is not the meaning of life in general," Frankl suggested "but rather the specific meaning of a person's life at a given moment." Meaning is not "invented" but rather "detected," he points out. We can discover meaning in life in three different ways: (1) by doing a deed; (2) by experience a value -- nature, a work of art, another person, love, etc., and (3) by suffering. Frankl discounts the effective utility of the Second Viennese School of Psychotherapy, i.e., Alfred Adler and his notion of humankind's "will-to-power," by arguing that personal power in the face of suffering and in the absence of personal meaning has no visible function within the personality (Frankl, 1962b).

A concept of humanity is held, consciously or not, by every school of psychotherapy (Morgan, 2012). We see it in Freud, Adler, and Jung, and so likewise with Frankl. That concept of the human person, suggests Frankl, affects everything, all conceptual development, all theories of treatment, all clinical perceptions. Resulting from his wartime concentration camp experience, Frankl became convinced of the *sui generus* nature of the will-to-meaning, what he later developed as logotherapy (Frankl, 1958). We must elevate this concept of the person for critical analysis from the logotherapeutic perspective if we ever hope to understand the differences in psychotherapeutic modalities of treatment. "For," explains Frankl, "a psychotherapist's concept of man ... can reinforce the patient's neurosis and, therefore, can be wholly nihilistic." For Frankl, there are three fundamental characteristics of human existence which converge to define the human person, namely, spirituality, freedom, and responsibility. This tripartite foundation inevitably affects every attempt to understand who we are and what we are to do. Frankl labored hard and long for a philosophical structure to logotherapy, believing that any model of psychotherapeutic analysis and treatment must have a strong philosophical basis (Frankl, 1961b).

Neither a proponent nor an opponent of a faith-based worldview *per se*, Frankl simply intends for spirituality not to be tied up with a specific notion of religion. Where faith helps a person through the day, Frankl has no objection to it. Where religious worldview and ethos stifle, cripple, or delude an individual, Frankl is opposed to it. What Frankl means by "spirituality" as a fundamental component of human nature is man's capacity for a sense of awe, wonder, and mystery, even reverence, in one's assessing the meaning, value, and purpose of one's own personal life. The surprising feature about Frankl's psychotherapeutic formulations is that throughout he consistently makes inferential comments about the religious dynamic operative in his own theory while constantly omitting any specific reference to its fundamentally Jewish character (Frankl, 1957; 1961a). The connectedness of all things as experienced in moments of high sensitivity or even ecstasy is the role spirituality plays in the human character. A deeply felt sense of beauty, power, and wonder in the universe, a heightened experience of integrality, what I have in another place chosen to call "systemic integrality," constitutes what spirituality means in logotherapy (Morgan, 2009). "By helping prisoners then and patients later remember their past lives – their joys, sorrows, sacrifices, and blessings – he emphasized the "meaningfulness" of their lives as already lived (Frankl,1954)." Whether one is a theist, an atheist, or an agnostic, Frankl contends that the dynamics of spirituality can be equally and meaningfully operate within a person's life bringing value and purpose.

Complimenting this sense of spirituality within the logotherapeutic model is a freedom which functions in the face of three things: (1) the instincts; (2) inherited disposition; and (3) environment. Frankl engages in a long and definitive discussion of freedom in his celebrated classic, *The Doctor and the Soul*, owing no doubt to his own personal encounter with the existential vacuum during his trying experiences in captivity. The converging of these three components of instincts, heredity, and environment constitutes the matrix out of which the human experience of freedom can grow and thrive in a person's life. To rise above one's instincts, says Frankl, is a distinctively human possibility and, unlike Freud's obsession with the power of instincts governing human behavior, Frankl specifically calls upon the responsible person to take his instincts in hand, use them but control them, for service to others. Likewise with heritage, one cannot deny one's own genetic composition but in the acknowledging of it one asserts power over its domination. A determinist, Frankl was most certainly not. He believed in the human person's ability to respond responsibly to self-knowledge. He emphasizes not only the recollected past, but calls attention to the existential meaningfulness of suffering and tragedy in life as testimonies to human courage and dignity (Frankl, 1961c). By knowing one's instincts and one's genetic heritage comes a source of strength and power to control, direct, and utilize the primordial nature of these characteristics for the good of self and humanity.

Finally, Frankl was not a member of the "nurture" crowd of behavioral psychologists who would attribute, even blame, one's social and physical environment for the way individuals turn out in their maturity. These three fundamental components of freedom, namely, instincts, heritage, and environment, may be used by the human person to realize freedom if he becomes aware of them, embraces them, and directs them towards a meaningful purpose in life. In logotherapy, Frankl differentiates meaning and values. Values are socially held meanings whereas "meaning as the *sine qua non* of life is a unique experience and possession of every single individual in every moment of one's own life (Frankl, 1961d)."

Besides spirituality and freedom, however, there is responsibility. Having been greatly influenced in his formative years with the writings of the existentialists, not least being Kierkegaard, Sartre, and Heidegger, Frankl was most insistent that in order for a person to be fully human, he must exercise responsibility. The individual is responsible to his own conscience first and foremost, says Frankl. Conscience, he suggests, is a "thing in itself," it is *sui generis*. It is so fundamental to the human person that humanity cannot exist without it nor the human person remain human without it. Conscience has to do with the drive to do the right thing because it is the right thing to do. This is so fundamental to the human experience that without it neither humanity nor civilization itself could exist. Of course, the "origin" of conscience is a point of controversy and contention within the various schools of psychotherapy and depth psychology. The three schools of thought regarding the origins of ethics and moral behavior I have discussed at length elsewhere, first in my book *Naturally Good: A Behavioral History of Moral Development* (2005), and more specifically the three school as Ethical Theism, Ethical Humanism, and Ethical Naturalism in my book *Beyond Divine Intervention: The Biology of Right and Wrong* (2009).

More so with Frankl than with any other psychotherapist, the personal life story of each individual proved to be a major factor in the development of his own therapeutic system of theory and practice. Frankl contended that this will-to-meaning – as Freud argued for "pleasure" and Adler for "power" – pervades every secret recess of one's personal life. Meaning, he pointed out, can be found in any situation within which we find ourselves (Frankl, 1953). Freud's life, Adler's life, and Jung's life have all proven interesting and have in their own way shown how their life and work were integrated. But with Frankl, it is inconceivable to imagine logotherapy as a school of thought being produced in the absence of his concentration camp experience. The viability of his theory and the utility of his clinical practice both rely upon the life history of its creator. Frankl's relevance to contemporary treatment in therapeutic settings is becoming increasingly recognized and appreciated within a broad spectrum of clinical practice. The impact of his therapeutic system of theory and treatment has yet to reach its maximum level of influence in contemporary counseling circles but the establishment of the Graduate Center for Pastoral Logotherapy at the Graduate Theological Foundation under the direction of Dr. Ann Graber (Graber, 2004) constitutes a major leap forward in this development.

When logotherapy is applied to the geriatric patient, there is a challenge to transform the central concepts of the therapeutic practice to the life situation of the individual whose life has, for all practical purpose, already been lived. Believing that logotherapy has, indeed, something yet to offer the geriatric patient, it is imperative that the "will to meaning" not be only thought of as an agenda for future living but as a hermeneutic for "living in the moment." Existential episodes of happiness constitute what the clinician might imagine to be the practical application of logotherapy in dealing with older and elderly individuals (Morgan, 2006). Rather than seeking for that window of hope for the future which is so characteristic of this modality of therapeutic practice, the logotherapist must creatively search for "existential episodes of happiness," as I have chosen to call them, viz., remembered events in which the older person demonstrably attributes the experience of "happiness." This approach, rather than focusing upon hope, focuses upon memories, times past which bring a moment of reflective happiness now. The existential character of the remembered happy event constitutes the possibility for a treasure trove of episodic happiness vignettes bringing comfort to the elderly facing a limited future.

Illustrative of this existential moment or window of happiness is the case of Mrs. Williams, a nursing home patient in her mid-80s suffering from acute and near debilitating depression. Other complicating health issues included high blood pressure, diabetes, and arthritis. A retired librarian for some twenty-plus years, Mrs. Williams came to the nursing home after falling in her home where she lived alone. The decision was made for institutional care in conjunction with family members (all distant cousins as she was widowed with no children). In meeting with her over several sessions, the therapist struggled with finding the "door of happy memories" through which to follow Mrs. Williams. Finally, during the third clinical session, some passing reference was made to her childhood farm life and swimming with her girlfriends in the cow pond behind the barn. As this passing reference seemed to cause her to pause and smile as she was formulaically reciting her "life's story" to the therapist, it became clear to the observing therapist that she enjoyed the memory and might enjoy elaborating upon it. The result was a meandering recollection of her childhood experiences with her friends on the family farm which, she said, "I haven't thought of in years." Subsequent sessions always harped back to these happy memories and provided a substance to her solitary reflections beyond the therapy sessions.

Often, the geriatric patient needs assistance in conjuring these past episodes of happiness and the therapist then can employ what I have chosen to call "memory suggestions," viz., asking the individual to back track consciously in search of "illustrative events" in his or her life to which they themselves attribute a blissful and happy experience. However, an important key here for the therapist to keep in mind is "stress avoidance," that is, redirecting the individual away from remembered events in their past which clearly, by facial expression or voice intonation, suggest stress or anxiety or unhappiness (Morgan, 2010). Family history is quite frequently the source of these happiness episodes but the therapist is advised to watch carefully lest the family history stories drift downward into negative memories.

It is crucial that the therapist keep in mind the logotherapeutic agenda lest one imagine that the purpose and goal of the therapeutic session is to search out the "meaning and purpose of life" yet to be lived. With the older and elderly patient, the acutely practical nature of the existential utility and viability of therapy must always be kept in the forefront of the therapeutic encounter when employing logotherapeutic analysis. Though sometimes a challenge in dealing with the elderly (geriatric dementia often manifests itself in the individual's disinclination to converse), the therapist must employ what I have chosen to call "points of conversation" as an impetus and incentive for the geriatric patient to engage the therapist in the quest for existential episodes of happiness (Morgan, 1987). Places, times, and people constitute for me the three fundamental arenas within which the patient may find these points of conversation leading to the "discovery" and "revisiting" of happiness episodes in their earlier life.

Another example of geriatric logotherapy is the case of Dr. Watson, a retired philosophy professor living alone in his home as a widower with two adult children living far away. Dr. Watson is in his late 80s, was once a nationally recognized scholar, author of several books, but these days finds reading increasingly difficult owing to glaucoma and writing virtually impossible due to arthritis in both hands. Reduced to sitting on his expansive front porch when weather permits and before the fireplace otherwise, Dr. Watson has sunk into a debilitating depression resulting in a consistent failure to eat regularly or to converse over the phone with friends and family. A concerned son precipitated the contact with a logotherapist who made an initial home visit, finding the above situation. Dr. Watson had essentially "given up," as he put it, because of an inability to read or write, his life's work and passion. When the therapist encouraged the professor to "tell me about your life's work," Dr. Watson commenced slowly and deliberately rattling off his educational background, teaching appointments, books written, conferences attended, all with little passion and near expressionless. However, when the therapist asked about specific colleagues mentioned in the monotone narrative, he noticed that the patient became somewhat animated, enthusiastic, even excited to relate story after story involving colleagues, happy stories, fun stories, all leading to an extremely productive journey through time and people of importance. Subsequent sessions centered upon the same topics with the results that Dr. Watson began calling old friends, inviting other retired colleagues in town to come for morning coffee and chat. The door of happy memories had been opened and entered and Dr. Watson's life took on renewed vitality.

One of the greatest challenges for the logotherapist is to acknowledge and own the inevitable reality of the brevity of life left to the elderly patient. The therapeutic goal here is clearly not some form of contrived "cure" for what might be the presenting symptoms of depression which is most commonly the driving force in seeking help for the patient either by the patient or the family or residential institutional staff responsible for caring for the patient. A cure certainly is not what is sought here, but rather, beyond and after the notion of a cure for the aged patient, there is an urgent need for the identification of the "rightful place for palliative care" in such situations. A quest for existential happiness, episodic joy from happy memories, constitutes the driving force in the therapeutic encounter with the geriatric patient who most commonly is suffering from depression.

A concluding illustration of the value of geriatric logotherapy and its use in existential counseling is the case of Miss Horton, an elderly spinster school teacher from a small town, whose life had been synonymous with teaching elementary school children, living in the background, watching them grow up, move away, establish families, and launch careers. Now nearly 90 years old residing in an assisted living facility in her little town, she had drifted into depression owing to a lack of social stimulus (most other residents were suffering from acute and severely debilitating geriatric dementia). Her health had declined gradually owing to heart problems and towards the end of her life, she had taken to the bed and less and less willing to converse with even the nurses. The nursing director called in the logotherapist (based on the therapist's reputation in dealing with geriatric dementia) and from the beginning the initial encounter was fruitless, boarding only hopeless. As the therapist explored Miss Horton's social life through interviews with nursing staff who knew the patient's personal history and in the therapist's search for the "magic door" that would introduce happy memories and reflective thoughts of joys gone by, it occurred to him that since her life had been lived for the children she taught, why not get some of those children, now adults, to come say goodbye to her in her closing days of life. It worked wonders. Through the local school, the therapist was able to contact several of her past students, now parents and successful people, to come for a visit. Since most people are uncomfortable visiting someone on their death bed, the therapist always arranged to be present, coaching the visitor to help Miss Horton "remember" episodes in the classroom and on the playground in which she was a major player and to share with her, as she lay mute but alert, the stories of their own lives as they left school and entered the world, always with reference to her contribution to their own personal lives. The results were remarkable, not that she lived much longer, for she did not, but during the closing weeks of her life, she became conversant, sitting up in bed, asking about this student and that student, remembering to the therapist more and more "happy moments" in her teaching life that brought a twinkle to her eyes and a smile on her face.

The practicality and professional humility of Viktor Frankl is evidenced in his quick and ready willingness to acknowledge the therapeutic limits of logotherapy, never claiming it to be a comprehensive analytical modality for all types of mental illness. Unlike other schools of thought which too frequently presume to be the panacea for all mental disorders, logotherapy has self-consciously identified its arenas of success and knows those in which it has little or no value. The distinctions center around psychogenic and biogenic classifications. Certainly and with little contradiction, logotherapy has a long clinical history of effective use in the treatment of psychogenic depression. When applied to the treatment of the elderly, not as a curative but as a palliative therapy, there is a promise great success. When it is not hope for the future which is being sought but rather an effective and celebrative address to the existential realities confronting the elderly patient who is facing decline and death, the quest for those "happy moments" conjured in the patient's memory constitute a promising field of treatment. Geriatric logotherapy is uniquely constructed to do just that.

END NOTES:

Viktor Frankl: Primary Sources

(1953) "Logos and Existence in Psychotherapy," *American Journal of Psychotherapy,* VII: 8-15.

(1954) "Group Psychotherapeutic Experiences in a Concentration Camp," *Group Psychotherapy,* VII: 81-90.

(1957) "The Spiritual Dimension in Existential Analysis and Logotherapy," *Journal of Individual Psychology,* XV: 157-165.

(1958) "The Will to Meaning," *The Journal of Pastoral Care,* XII: 82-88.

(1961a) "Religion and Existential Psychotherapy," *The Gordon Review,* VI: 2-10.

(1961b) "Psychotherapy and Philosophy," *Philosophy Today,* v: 59-64.

(1961c) "Logotherapy and the Challenge of Suffering," *Review of Existential Psychology and Psychiatry,* I: 3-7.

(1961d) "Dynamics, Existence and Values," *Journal of Existential Psychiatry,* II: 5-16.

(1962a) "Psychiatry and Man's Quest for Meaning," *Journal of Religion and Health,* I:93-103.

(1962b) "Logotherapy and the Challenge of Suffering," *Pastoral Psychology,* XIII:25-28.

(1963). *Man's Search for Meaning. An Introduction to Logotherapy.* Boston: Beacon Press.

(1967). *Psychotherapy and Existentialism: Selected Papers on Logotherapy.* New York: Simon & Schuster.

(1969). *The Will to Meaning: Foundations and Applications of Logotherapy.* New York: New American Library.

(1997). *Man's Search for Ultimate Meaning.* New York: Basic Books

(2001). *Man's Search for Ultimate Meaning: A Psychology Exploration of the Religious Quest.* (With a Foreword by Swanee Hunt). MJF Books.

(2004). *On the Theory and Therapy of Mental Disorders: An Introduction to Logotherapy and Existential Analysis.* (James M. DuBois, Trans.). London: Routledge.

Secondary Sources

(2004) Graber, Ann V. *Viktor Frankl's Logotherapy: Method of Choice in Ecumenical Pastoral Psychology* (2nd ed.). Lima, OH: Wyndham Hall Press.

(1987) Morgan, John H. *From Freud to Frankl: Our Modern Search for Personal Meaning.* Bristol, IN: Wyndham Hall Press.

(2005) Morgan, John H. *Naturally Good: A Behavioral History of Moral Development* (South Bend, IN: Cloverdale Books).

(2006) Morgan, John H. *Being Human: Perspectives on Meaning and Interpretation (Essays in Religion, Culture and Personality)* (2nd ed.). South Bend, IN: Cloverdale Books.

(2009) Morgan, John H. *Beyond Divine Intervention: The Biology of Right and Wrong.* Lima, OH: Wyndham Hall Press.

(2010) Morgan, John H. *Clinical Pastoral Psychotherapy: A Practitioner's Handbook for Ministry Professionals.* Mishawaka, IN: Graduate Theological Foundation.

(2012) Morgan, John H. *Beginning With Freud: The Classical Schools of Psychotherapy* (Expanded 2nd Edition). Lima, OH: Wyndham Hall Press.

CHAPTER SIX
Medication and Counseling in Psychiatric Practice: Biogenic Psycho-pharmacology and Psychogenic Psychotherapy

(Partnering in the Treatment of Mental Illness)

The practice of psychiatry, though a very young specialization within the field of medicine, was historically restricted to practitioners holding the Doctor of Medicine degree. It covered a wide ranging field of interests and clinical practices, including but not restricted to a combination of psychotropic drugs and psychotherapy. Since the coming of Harry Stack Sullivan (1892-1949), psychiatry has been redefined by him and his colleagues at the William Alanson White Institute of Psychiatry in New York City and the Washington School of Psychiatry in D.C. as "the study of processes that involve or go on between people. The field of psychiatry," then, he suggested, "is the field of interpersonal relations, under any and all circumstances in which these relations exist." Not everyone in or out of medical practice agree with Sullivan and his colleagues but the sentiment within the broader counseling professions is that this more expansive and psychogenic definition is now more commonly employed in today's complex world of clinical psychotherapeutic and medical practice than is the old traditional and restricted biogenic definition circumscribed by psychotropic medical intervention.

Medication and counseling, and a varying combination of the two, constitute what today is thought of as the appropriate treatment of mental illness. Based on whether the diagnosis of the presenting mental disorder is biogenic or psychogenic in nature, either psychotropic drugs or psychotherapy must necessarily dictate the treatment prescribed. Psychopharmacology and psychotherapy are both considered appropriate methods of treatment depending, of course, on the diagnosis. The present state of psychiatry, dominated by the insurance industry's jurisdiction in terms of coverable fee-based treatment, has been somewhat restricted in the use of psychotherapy in deference to psychopharmacological intervention. Within and without the profession there is the general consensus that the practice of psychiatry has suffered from these fiscal constraints and, therefore, a reliance upon social workers trained in counseling has become the normative practice within psychiatric treatment when a psychogenic illness has been diagnosed.

If Sullivan and company's expanded definition of psychiatry is embraced, namely, that this field of medicine deals fundamentally with interpersonal relationships, and the medical community is in agreement that both drugs and counseling are appropriate modalities of treatment, based upon the diagnosis, then a companioning of psychopharmacology and psychotherapy in psychiatric practice seems most reasonable and desirable. Biogenic illnesses are subject to psychopharmacological treatment whereas psychogenic illnesses are the domain of psychotherapy. In the best of all possible worlds, a complimentary relationship of these two modalities of treatment constitutes the ideal situation in any clinical practice. One need not adhere to the extremism of Thomas Szasz to see the value in pursuing a balanced diagnosis and treatment of mental illness using both drugs and counseling. The exploration of both modalities of treatment, pointing out the value of each within their own perimeters of jurisdiction and practice, would constitute a significant contribution to the discussion of the relationship between medication and counseling in the treatment of mental illness and the nurturing of mental health.

CHAPTER SEVEN
A Tribute to Carl Rogers' Celebrated Classic *On Becoming a Person (1961)*

Carl Rogers (1902-1987), though he wrote much and often, established himself on the basis of two major works, namely, *Client-Centered Therapy: Its Current Practice, Implications, and Theory* (1951) and *On Becoming a Person: A Therapist's View of Psychotherapy* (1961). Roger's first and overriding characteristic in the writing of his first major book was to emphasize the warmth and acceptance of the counseling relationship between the counselor and the client. His first major book was meant to emphasize the new rationale of his approach, namely, "The client, as the term has acquired its meaning, is one who comes actively and voluntarily to gain help on a problem, but without any notion of surrendering his own responsibility for the situation" (1951:17). From non-directive counseling to client-centered counseling to, finally, person-to-person therapy, Rogers' thought has continued to grow and expand. Yet, his initial entry into the cauldron of psychotherapeutic theorizing in his first book (1951) to his major opus of 1961 finally culminating in his later work all bespeak of his capacity to grow through learning in the clinical environment. He gradually came to realize that the relationship between therapist and client is the most important aspect underlying personality change. Herein lay his interest and this is where he concentrated the bulk of his entire career (1942).

Rogers brought to the psychotherapeutic table a new way of seeing the counselor's role in relationship to the client (1980). He suggested that the emphasis shift should be from an objectified standoffish posture to an empathic approach in understanding the client's world, and then the therapist should seek to communicate that understanding directly to the client. In mirroring back to the client the feelings the counselor pick up on in the interview encounter, the counselor simultaneously transmitted the desire to perceive the world as the client perceives it, thus, leading to the role of non-directivity in the dyadic relationship. Rogers insisted that the counselor's role was to achieve an internal frame-of-reference with the client. "It is the counselor's aim," says Rogers, "to perceive as sensitively and accurately as possible all of the perceptual field as it is being experienced by the client … and having thus perceived this internal frame of reference of the other as completely as possible, to indicate to the client the extent to which he is seeming through the client's eyes" (1961:43)

In this new psychotherapy, Rogers emphasized four important principles. First, the new therapy "relies much more heavily on the individual drive toward growth, health, and adjustment. Therapy is not a matter of doing something to the individual, or of inducing him to do something about himself. It is instead a matter of freeing him for normal growth and development" (1961:59). Second, "this new therapy places greater stress upon the emotional elements, the feelings aspects of the situation, than upon the intellectual aspects." Third, "this new therapy places greater stress upon the immediate situation than upon the individual's past." And, fourth, this new approach "lays great stress upon the therapeutic relationship itself as a growth experience.

Here, explains Rogers, " the individual learns to understand himself; to make significant independent choices, to relate himself successfully to another person in a more adult fashion." Rogers firmly believed that individual, by and large had it within themselves to solve their own problems (1967b). The task, then, of the therapist in Rogers' view was to establish the conditions which would allow individuals to attain this insight for themselves. Attainment of insight was, therefore, one of the key goals of nondirective therapy. On the other hand, the counselor's chief task was to reach the "clarification of feelings" through rephrasing the emotional content of the client's statements such that the client gains a new insight into his own stated condition. "Effective counseling," says Rogers, "consists of a definitively structured, permissive relationship which allows the client to gain an understanding of himself to a degree which enables him to take positive steps in the light of his new orientation" (1961:31).

The three major elements characterizing Rogers' theory of personality were (1) the necessity for the counselor to provide a warm and permissive relationship for the client, (2) the necessity for the counselor to assume the internal frame of reference of the client and to communicate empathic understanding of the client's world, and (3) finally, to reach a mutual expression of feelings between the client and the counselor thereby realizing the full potential of the client-centered theory of personality and psychotherapeutic treatment. Rogers identified six conditions of client-counselor relationships which, if met, would constitute the basis for a successful therapy (1967a).

Rogers believed he had already proven clinically that a theoretical rationale for personality change in therapy was possible which implied that constructive alterations in personality could occur regardless of the specific verbal techniques employed by the counselor. He recited these six conditions to reinforce his theory. First, two persons are in psychological contact such that each of them is fully aware that the other's presence makes a difference. Second, the client is in a state of incongruence in relationship with the counselor due to a discrepancy between the client's self-image and his existential experience in the counseling environment. Third, the therapist is, on the other hand, congruent (which means integrated) in the relationship due to the pre-set definition of his role in the situation. Fourth, the therapist experiences unconditional positive regard for the client as this is crucial in order to establish a meaningful relationship in the counseling milieu. Fifth, the therapist experiences an empathic understanding of the client's internal frame of reference and endeavors to communicate this experience to the client such that the encounter proves therapeutically successful in direct correlation to the therapist's capacity to emote empathy. And, sixth and finally, the communication to the client of the therapist's empathic understanding and unconditional positive regard must be minimally achieved or, otherwise, no helpful therapeutic result will occur.

Rogers was a conspicuous member of the Third Force, the humanistic school of psychology which set itself *vis a vis* both to psychoanalysis and to behaviorism (Maslow, 1968; 1976). His understanding of human nature was, of course, central to his position as a leader in the Third Force movement. He speaks of the driving force in his work which is "the continuing clinical experience with individuals who perceive themselves, or are perceived by others to be, in need of personal help." "Since 1928, for a period now approaching thirty years," he wrote in 1958, "I have spent probably an average of 15 to 20 hours per week, except during vacation periods, in endeavoring to understand and be of therapeutic help to these individuals. From these hours, and from my relationships with these people, I have drawn most of whatever insight I possess into the meaning of therapy, the dynamics of interpersonal relationships, and the structure and function of personality." Rogers firmly believed that at their core, every human being is fundamentally good, being essentially purposive, forward-moving, constructive, realistic, and trustworthy (Morgan, 2011a). Because of this essential goodness of the human person, every individual, given the right opportunity for growth, love, and affirmation, will blossom forth in his own innate potential, optimum personal development and effectiveness (1951).

Christianity, Rogers argued, has nurtured a core belief in the innate evil of the human person, an inclination to evil and sin. Furthermore, he is unabashed in arguing that this demented notion of human nature has been influenced, even trumped, by Freud and the psychoanalytic school of psychotherapy. If permitted to run free from the scrutiny and domination of the ego and the superego, the human personality's unconscious id would manifest itself, according to Freud and Christians, in incest, homicide, thievery, rape, and other horrendous acts of self-destructive behavior (1980). People do engage in such behavior and this occurs when they have been stifled, been misdirected, or their natural personality development has been suppressed from its natural inclinations. When, however, people are able to function as fully human beings, when they are free to experience and express themselves, they show a positive and rational approach to life which elicits trust and nurtures harmony in interpersonal relationships.

Rogers protested against those cynical and jaded psychotherapists and theologians who thought of him as naïve and simplistic: "I do not have a Pollyanna view of human nature," he argued. "I am quite aware that out of defensiveness and inner fear individuals can and do behave in ways which are incredibly cruel, horribly destructive, immature, regressive, anti-social, and harmful. Yet, one of the most refreshing and invigorating parts of my experience is to work with such individuals and to discover the strongly positive directional tendencies which exist in them, as in all of us, at the deepest levels" (1977). This driving force in human nature towards the good and self-fulfilling he calls the actualizing tendency, and he believes it is latent in every human being. He defines it as "the inherent tendency of the organism (the personality) to develop all its capacities in ways which serve to maintain or enhance the person." Therefore, says he, the fundamental principle guiding every person's life is the drive to actualize, maintain, or enhance themselves, indeed, to become the best that their inherited natures will permit them to be. This is, essentially, the sole motivating principle in Roger's theory of personality (1954).

To be sure, there are certain definitive characteristics which establish this actualizing tendency. Let us explore them momentarily here. Of course and to begin with, says Rogers, there is a biological factor which is operative here, namely, this tendency is an inborn characteristic necessary to maintain the individual but also for the enhancement of the individual by providing a mechanism for the development and differentiation of the body's functions, growth, and development. But, of more importance than even this is the motivating force which the actualizing tendency provides for in increased autonomy and self-reliance in pursuit of the individual's full potential in life. Furthermore, the actualizing tendency is not merely for the reduction of tension in the stresses of one's physical or biological life, contrary to Freud's insistence on the prominence of instincts. Rather, the individual is motivated, says Rogers in an earlier work, by a growth process in which potentialities and capacities are brought to realization (1942). This actualizing tendency, then, says he, "is the essence of life itself."

The actualizing tendency, explains Rogers, serves as a criterion against which all of one's life experiences are evaluated and, particularly, when individuals engage in what he calls the "organism valuing process." This process involves the individual's overt effort in maintaining and enhancing the sought after and valued positive behaviors and experiences in life for they produce within the individual a strong feeling of satisfaction in the realization of one's full potential. This process is a mechanism for the evaluation, the weighing, the determining whether or not an experience is affirmative or negative to self-fulfillment (1946). And, the most critical aspect of this actualizing tendency, says Rogers, is the individual's drive toward self-actualization, what he has called the "self-actualizing tendency." This particular tendency, then, is what gives a forward thrust to life, to the individual who must encounter and incorporate life's complexities as well as its self-sufficiencies and its maturation processes. Self-actualization, then, is the process of becoming a more adequate person.

Rogers counted himself among the phenomenologists of the day who were practicing humanistic psychology as members of the Third Force (Morgan, 2010). The Third Force was never a formal body but consisted of humanistic psychologists who pushed their worldview as a viable alternative to Freud and Skinner, or psychoanalysis and behaviorism, in both theory and practice (1968). Phenomenological psychology contends that the psychological reality of the individual's world is exclusively a function of the way in which the world is perceived by that individual. The truth does not really matter because it can never really be identified. What really matters to the individual is what that person thinks is true, sees to be true, acts in relationship to what he sees and thinks to be the truth. Phenomenological psychology argues that what is real to an individual, that is, what reality is thought, understood, or felt to be, is that which exists within that person's internal frame of reference. It is this frame of reference which is important in the psychotherapeutic relationship. Rogers was insistent upon this point, namely, that every individual interprets his world and that interpretation is that with which the therapist must comes to grips. The only way to understand an individual's behavior and attitude is to come to an understanding of this internal frame of reference. It is the subjective reality of the client's perceived world which is important, not the objective truth (Morgan, 2011b).

Needless to say, Rogers' identification with the phenomenological approach to personality theory is based upon his strong conviction that the complexity of human behavior can only be understood within the context of the whole person. His emphasis upon the holistic view of personality, namely, that the person reacts as an integrated organism and that his unity cannot be derived from mere behaviorism, is at the core of his therapy. It is the self which constitutes the focus of his analysis for it is the fundamental center of human personality. His theory of personality development is based upon this conviction (1961). "The self, or self-concept," says Rogers, "is defined as an organized, consistent, conceptual gestalt composed of perceptions of the characteristics of the 'I' or 'me' to others and to various aspects of life, together with the values attached to these perceptions. It is a gestalt which is available to awareness though not necessarily in awareness." The self-concept is comprised of (1) what the individual thinks he is, (2) what he thinks he ought to be, and (3) and the ideal self or what he thinks he would like to be. This tripartite composition of the self constitutes the core of Rogers' personality theory.

Rogers does not believe that the self *per se* manages and monitors the individual's behavior but rather it symbolizes the individual's conscious experiences of the world -- who he thinks he is, who he thinks he ought to be, and who he thinks he wants to be. He discounts, not the reality of unconscious data, but its relevance to the individual's self-concept and its viability in the therapeutic situation for it is the individual's own self-understanding, as he explains it, describes it, characterizes it, that is important therapeutically. Phenomenology trumps unconscious data as the basis for psychological therapy, says Rogers, for the structure of the self is formed through the individual's interaction with the familial, social, and cultural environment (1951). The "content of one's self-concept," argued Rogers, "is fundamentally a social product and not the result of the bombardment of the psyche with unconscious and repressed data."

Therefore, there are identifiable components needed for the development of a healthy self-concept and when they are absent or twisted from experience, the individual suffers. First, Rogers suggests that every person has a basic desire for warmth, respect, admiration, love, and acceptance from people important in his life. He calls this the "need for positive regard." Whether innate or socially learned, this drive is strong from the earliest days of childhood (1969). Rogers believes a person, whether infant, child, adolescent, or adult, will do almost anything to meet this innate need for positive regard. There is a reciprocal component to this drive as well, namely, in the giving of this positive regard, one receives it in turn. The reciprocity of positive regard is a strong re-enforcer of social relationships. The self, says Rogers, is profoundly influenced by this need and rather than suggest that individuals are driven to satisfy the demands and expectations of their self-concept, he argues that people are driven to satisfy their need for positive regard, both to give it and to receive it. Where there is a conflict between what the individual's wants in service to his self and what he recognizes as in service to his need for regard, Rogers calls "incongruence." "This, as we see it, is the basic estrangement in man. He has not been true to himself, to his own natural organism valuing of experience, but for the sake of preserving the positive regard of others has now come to falsify some of the values he experiences and to perceive them only in terms based upon their value to others" (1961:89). The conflict internally, that is, incongruency, is the result of the individual choosing to service his need for positive regard at the expense of serving his own self's perceived personal needs. The conflict often leads to psychological stress, tension, and mental illness. "Yet," Rogers continues, "this has not been a conscious choice, but a natural -- and tragic -- development in infancy. The path of development toward psychological maturity is the undoing of this estrangement in man's functioning as the achievement of a self which is congruent with experience, and the restoration of a unified organism valuing process as the regulator of behavior." Too often, it is the people pleaser who emerges from this incongruity, the individual who is so drives to please the other person that he forgets to please himself in the process (1981).

Within the context of self-concept development within every individual from childhood is the presence of what Rogers called "conditional positive regard," namely, that situation in the family and society in which the individual is the recipient of positive regard only so long as that individual conforms to the expectations of the positive regard provider. In other words, positive regard is contingent upon compliance with outside expectations of family and society members. "I will love you so long as," or "only if" situations constitute conditional positive regard. This situation, Rogers believes, is detrimental to the child becoming a fully functioning and self-actualized individual (1972). The child, and eventually the adult, relinquishes ownership of his own needs and desires in order to conform to the conditions laid out by the parent, the family, and society for the giving of positive regard. The individual runs the serious risk of "losing himself" to himself in the process of conforming to the conditions established by others for the giving of positive regard. This condition of worth is compliance with the expectations of others, regardless of one's own sense of what is valued. This was painfully true in Rogers' own personal life as a child raised in an extremely restrictive religious home environment (Kirchenbaum, 1979).

To counter act the mental health dangers of conditional positive regard, Rogers developed the concept of unconditional positive regard, and this concept characterizes all of his psychotherapeutic practice and theorizing about psychological treatment. In light of his own childhood experience, Rogers developed this concept as a counterpoise to the detrimental character of the conditions of worth operative in conditional positive regard. He believed strongly that it is possible to give and receive positive regard without attaching it to behavioral compliance. Positive regard can be given to individuals in situations where the behavior of the other individual is not necessarily to the liking of the positive regard giving individual (1970). This requires every individual to be accepted and respected for who and what they are, without conditions of ifs, ands, or buts. Such unconditional positive regard is most evident in a mother's love of a misbehaving child. Parental love is not, then, given to the child when and only when the child conforms to the parents' behavioral expectations but love, positive regard, is given unconditionally. Rogers was quick to criticize the Christian saying from Jesus, "You are my friends if you do what so ever I tell you." This is conditional worth and not love and it can and usually is damaging to the child and the adult as well.

Rogers believes that if children were raised in the unconditional positive regard familial environment, "then no conditions of worth would develop, self-regard would be unconditional, the needs for positive regard and self-regard would never be at variance with organism evaluation, and the individual would continue to be psychologically adjusted, and would be fully functioning. This chain of evens is hypothetically possible, and hence important theoretically, though it does not appear to occur in actuality" (1969). Discipline is not absent from the family environment, but the circumstances under which it is used and understood by child and parent are radically different because it is disassociated from self-worth. The creation of an unconditional love atmosphere provides the mechanism for a positive use of discipline wherein the child can grow into a fully functioning and potentially self-actualized person with a deep and unchallenged sense of self worth.

Growing out of Rogers' understanding of the nature

of the experience of incongruity were the experiences of threat, anxiety, and defense. These three very common experiences are all interrelated and are manifested in the presence of the individual's awareness or lack of awareness in an incongruous situation. Every individual strives for what Rogers calls "consistency in behavior," attempting at all times to keep an even keel in interpersonal relationships based upon the individual's self-concept. Where there is an incongruity between the individual's self-concept and the social situation making demands upon him inconsistent with his idea of himself, that individual feels a threat. The threat in Rogers' theory occurs when a person recognizes an incongruity between his self-concept and its corollary condition of worth and the experience which precipitates the incongruity. This threatening situation is not always self-evidently conscious but the individual feels anxious by the encounter (1946). Whenever this experience of incongruity exists in the individual's encounter where self-concept and outside experience are at odds, the individual feels a sense of vulnerability and often personality disorganization. Anxiety is, then, an emotional response to a threat to the individual's self-concept such that there is real danger of a debilitating discrepancy between the person and the situation.

When this situation arises, namely, a perceived conflict between self-concept and objective situation, the individual attempts to protect himself by the use of a defense mechanism. The process of defense, explains Rogers, is the behavioral response of the individual to the threat and the goal is for the reestablishment and maintenance of the self-concept. "This goal," Rogers continues, "is achieved by the perceptual distortion of the experience in awareness, in such a way as to reduce the incongruity between the experience and the structure of the self, or by the denial of any experience, thus denying any threat to the self" (1961:107). The production of defenses, then, is the individual's primary method of protecting himself, his self-concept, and his self-worth.

These defense mechanisms are of two kinds, says Rogers. There is the perceptual distortion and the denial. The first occurs when an incongruent experience is allowed into an individual's perception but only in a form that makes it consistent with that individual's self-image and not something alien to his own experience. Thus, when an experience occurs challenging the individual but not outside the sphere of possibility, that individual employs a defense mechanism to explain the distortion in the experience rather than denying its reality. This occurs when someone is caught stealing when that individual is aware that even though he is not habitually a thief it can, does, and might happen that he takes something that is really not his. This often occurs with employees of a company who help themselves to various items, aware that it is theft, but explaining to their own satisfaction that it is acceptable behavior. This, Rogers calls, "rationalization." Perceptual distortion produces rationalization thereby allowing an individual to maintain his self-concept without any or much jeopardy. However, in the case of denial as a defense mechanism, the individual attempts to protect their self-concept by simply denying that the situation of incongruity has occurred (1939). When this defense mechanism, much more so than the previous one, is permitted to reign in a person's life, there is grave potential for the development of mental illness.

Throughout his writing career, Rogers made much of what he called the good life in which he used a specific term for that experience, namely, the fully functioning person. The good life, for Rogers, is not a static state of experience, but a process, a direction, a way of living and comporting oneself through all of life's trials and tribulations. The good life "is a process of movement in a direction which the human organism selects when it is inwardly free to move in any direction. The general qualities of this selected direction appear to have a certain universality," Rogers contends, and "the person who is psychologically free moves in the direction of becoming a more fully functioning person" (1961:79). There are five major personality traits of such individuals and we will recite them briefly here. (1) Openness to experience (wherein the individual is not temperamentally closed to new situations, encounters, opportunities, challenges), (2) Existential living (wherein the individual is ready and willing to face what ever may come his way with hope, courage, and fortitude), (3) Organismic trusting (wherein the individual has confidence in his ability to make sound decisions and to act upon them with assurance of their wisdom), (4) Experiential freedom (wherein the individual embraces the possibilities of life without false or shallow constraints superimposed by family and society but with a willingness to explore possibilities for living), and (5) Creativity (wherein the individual is fully at liberty to venture into new realms of experiential living and expressiveness of life's possibilities). "The good life," Rogers expounds, "involves a wider range, a greater richness, than the constricted living in which most of us find ourselves. To be a part of this process means that one is involved in the frequently frightening and frequently satisfying experience of a more sensitive living, with greater range, greater variety, greater richness" (1977).

The juxtaposition of Rogerian psychology and that of Freud and Skinner is most profoundly realized in their differences over the nature of the human person. The Third Force school of humanistic psychology was intentionally launched to counter the negativity and pessimism of both Freud's determinism and Skinner's behaviorism (Maslow, 1976). Eight distinguishing traits are counterpoised in these schools of thought with Rogers and the phenomenological humanists on the one hand and the psychoanalysts and behaviorists on the other. First is that of freedom versus determinism, with Rogers strongly for the former and Freud and Skinner quite conspicuously on the side of the latter. Freedom, for Rogers, is an indispensable characteristic of human nature and without it the fully functioning individual has no chance of self-actualization. Again, rationality versus irrationality characterizes the radical distinction between these schools of thought (Morgan, 2010). For Rogers, the human person is essentially a rational being, controlling and directing his own life when given the opportunity and, with help, can correct misdirection in one's life in a way that Freud and Skinner could never conceive nor would they allow. Holism, for Rogers, is his alternative to behaviorism's elementalism, by which is meant the behaviorist's happy dissecting of the human personality into elemental parts for analysis whereas with the humanists the person is treated and respected as an entity in its entirety.

A further distinction has to do with the difference between constitutionalism and environmentalism, with the former on the side of the humanists who would have us know that individuals are constituted of an innate tendency to self-actualization whereas the behaviorists would have us rely upon the organic and instinctual situation of the individual as determinate in behavior. Whereas Skinner and Freud would emphasize the objectivity of the human person's behavioral modalities of being without reference to the individual's own self-understanding, Rogers would have us know that the human person is essentially a subjective being with thought processes and behavioral modalities employed at his own initiative and to his own desired ends. Again, Rogers would have us understand that the human person is "proactive" rather than "reactive" to life's situations and that the positive view of the human person is one in which every individual has the ability and is encouraged to assume responsibility for his actions rather than rely helplessly upon his instinctual urges and unconscious cuing for behavioral responses. We are a proactive being rather than a mere reactive animal say the humanists of the Third Force.

Because human beings are innately driven toward self-actualization, every individual is heterostatic rather than homeostatic, that is to say, every person is in a mode of action, moving towards greater fulfillment, greater self-actualization, rather than bond and gagged by the instinctual and unconscious variables operative in his life but outside his control. Man is moving forward, not staked to his mere animal confines. And, finally, Roger would emphasize knowability whereas the behaviorists would claim unknowability as our life situation and destiny. Because of his embracing of the phenomenological school of psychology, Roger believed that man cannot use scientific knowledge to better understand who and what we are without a much greater reliance upon our own capacity at self-understanding. We are not merely the objective subject of scientific enquiry, but we are the subjective focus of interpersonal self-understanding. Science can help, but it must serve rather than dominate our enquiry.

Early on in our discussion, we called attention to the evolution of Rogerian psychotherapeutic methods of treatment, moving from a non-directive to client-centered to finally person-to-person center focus. In this context, Rogers has identified six conditions necessary for the therapeutic relationship to be beneficial. In closing, we will itemize these and comment briefly. (1) Two persons are in psychological contact (wherein two individuals, one self-defined as therapist and the other as client, meet together to address a personal issue of the client); (2) The client is in a state of incongruence, being vulnerable or anxious (wherein the situation presumes an interactive relationship of the two individuals addressing the incongruent feelings of the client), (3) The therapist is congruent or integrated in the relationship (by which is meant that this individual is aware of his role, his situation, and his responsibility in relationship to the client), (4) The therapist experiences unconditional positive regard for the client (such that the client does not raise defenses and is rather openly convergent with the therapist about his situation of anxiety), (5) The therapist experiences an empathic understanding of the client's internal frame of reference and endeavors to communicate this experience to the client (such that the client is enabled to better see and assess the situation which has arisen in his life which has produced the incongruence), and (6) The communication to the client of the therapist's empathic understanding and unconditional positive regard is to a minimal degree achieved (thereby setting the client on the road to recovering or discovering a sense of self-worth and fulfillment).

Roger's person-to-person therapeutic method is a reflection of his whole image of man in general and more specifically of the therapist as a facilitator of personal growth of the client towards self-actualization. Believing individuals are innately inclined to personal fulfillment and, therefore, Rogers is ever optimistic about the healing process. His phenomenological theory has produced a great deal of research dealing with self-concept and his methodology has been widely adopted by various schools of psychotherapy, and not least within the ranks of pastoral counselors who have benefited the most and utilized his method extensively in their training and practice. On the occasion of the jubilee year of the publication of his now classic text, *On Becoming a Person*, it seems only appropriate that we pause in gratitude for his great contribution to an understanding of the development of the human person.

REFERENCES

Kirchenbaum, Howard (1979) On Becoming Carl

Rogers (N.Y.: Delacorte Press).

Maslow, Abraham (1968) *Toward a Psychology of Being* (N.Y.: Penguin).

Morgan, John H. (2010) *Beginning With Freud: The Classical Schools of Psychotherapy* (Lima, OH: Wyndham Hall Press).

Morgan, John H. (2011) *Psychology of Religion: A Commentary on the Classic Texts* (Lima, OH: Wyndham Hall Press).

Morgan, John H. (2013) *Understanding Self and Society: Leading Theorists in the History and Philosophy of the Social Sciences* (Lima, OH: Wyndham Hall Press, forthcoming 2013).

Rogers, Carl R. (1942) *Counseling and Psychotherapy: Newer Concepts in Practice*. Boston: Houghton Mifflin Company.

Rogers, Carl R., and John L. Wallen. (1946) *Counseling with Returned Servicemen*. New York: McGraw-Hill Book Company, Inc.

Rogers, Carl R. (1951) *Client-Centered Therapy: Its Current Practice, Implications, and Theory*. Boston: Houghton Mifflin.

Rogers, Carl R., and Rosalind F. Dymond, eds. (1954) *Psychotherapy and Personality Change: Coordinated Research Studies in the Client-Centered Approach*. Chicago: University of Chicago Press.

Rogers, Carl R. (1961) *On Becoming a Person: A*

Therapist's View of Psychotherapy. Boston: Houghton Mifflin.

Rogers, Carl R., and Barry Stevens. (1967a) *Person to Person: the Problem of Being Human: A New Trend in Psychology.* Walnut Creek, CA: Real People Press.

Rogers, Carl R., E. T. Gendlin, D. J. Kiesler, and C. B. Truax, eds. (1967b) *The Therapeutic Relationship and Its Impact: A Study of Psychotherapy with Schizophrenics.* Madison: University of Wisconsin Press.

Rogers, Carl R., and William R. Coulson, eds. (1968) *Man and the Science of Man.* Columbus, Ohio: Charles E. Merrill Publishing Company.

Rogers, Carl R. (1969) *Freedom to Learn: A View of What Education Might Become.* Columbus, Ohio: Charles E. Merrill Publishing Company.

Rogers, Carl R. (1970) *Carl Rogers on Encounter Groups.* New York: Harper and Row.

Rogers, Carl R. (1972) *Becoming Partners: Marriage and Its Alternatives.* New York: Delacorte Press.

Rogers, Carl R. (1977) *Carl Rogers on Personal Power: Inner Strength and Its Revolutionary Impact.* New York: Delacorte Press.

Rogers, Carl R. (1980) *A Way of Being.* Boston: Houghton-Mifflin.

Rogers, Carl C. and Lyon, H.C., Jr.. (1981) *On Becoming a Teacher.* Columbus, OH: Merill Publishers.

Rogers, Carl R. (1983) *Freedom to Learn for the 80s.*
Columbus, Ohio: Charles E. Merrill Publishing Company.

CHAPTER EIGHT
Psychology of Religion and the Books that Made it Happen

Between William James' 1902 *The Varieties of Religious Experience* and Peter Homans' 1970 *Theology After Freud*, the field of the psychology of religion was born and grew to maturity. About that, there is no serious question or doubt (Beit-Hallahmi; Coe; Gargiulo; Kendler; Strunk).. Within these seven decades, a discipline came into existence and established itself irrevocably as an indispensable component of the study of the human person. Under the influence of James' pioneering work and culminating in the provocative work of Homans, twelve books proved pivotal in the emergence of the psychology of religion as a respected area of research, study, and specialization within both the disciplines of psychology and theology. Of course, any number of scholars will wish to argue with the selection of these twelve titles but few will argue against the merits of those selected here. Another twelve could be named and another, but these have been chosen as indicative of the consensus within the academy of their crucial relevance to this collection honoring William James' life and work commemorating the centennial of his death in 1910 (Richardson 2006).

It might prove helpful to the reader for there to be a simple listing of the twelve titles selected for consideration here and then, following a brief acknowledgement and assessment of Edwin D. Starbuck's 1899 Scribner's publication, *Psychology of Religion*, wherein the term "psychology of religion" was used for the first time, we will proceed with our assessment of each book and its relevance to the development of the field of study called the psychology of religion. The twelve titles which constitute the consensus among the scholars surveyed are as follows

116

and they are listed and considered in chronological order of publication.

(English Translation dates used where relevant)

James, William (1902) *The Varieties of Religious Experience*
Leuba, James H. (1915) *Psychological Origin and Nature of Religion*
Freud, Sigmund (1927) *The Future of an Illusion*
Jung, Carl (1938) *Psychology and Religion*
Roberts, David E. (1950) *Psychotherapy and A Christian View of Man*
Allport, Gordon (1950) *The Individual and His Religion*
Fromm, Eric (1950) *Psychoanalysis and Religion*
Rank, Otto (1950) *Psychology and the Soul*
Bakan, David (1958) *Sigmund Freud and the Jewish Mystical Tradition*
Erikson, Erik (1958) *Young Man Luther: A Study in Psychoanalysis and History*
Maslow, Abraham (1970) *Religion, Values, and Peak-Experiences*
Homans, Peter (1970) *Theology After Freud*

Clearly this collection and the timeframe covered by their publication can be divided into a three-step development, namely, from James to Jung (1092 to 1938), from Roberts the Rank (1950) which constituted the backbone of the discipline's development, and from Bakan to Humans (1958-1970), when Freud comprised the beginning and ending of the third step. James, Leuba, Freud, and Jung were adventurers in the field of the psychology of religion, exploring where no one had ventured before and attempting an analysis that others would have understandably shied away from given the problematic of the subject matter. Religion was not to be tampered with during this time period except ever so gingerly. But on the shoulders of the four pioneers of James, Leuba, Freud, and Jung, Roberts, Allport, Fromm, and Rank were at liberty to explore the practical applications of their forebears' insights, speculations, and expostulations. These four, then, launched a monolithic barrage of investigations and applications the likes of which had never been imagined before and the likes of which will not be seen again as a single moment in time. Finally, and upon the shoulders of the second generation of adventurers, the four members of the third step, i.e., Bakan, Erikson, Maslow, and Homans, chose to address the insights of their predecessors relative to Freud and psychoanalysis in a manner that once and for all introduced the viability and effectiveness of the discipline of the psychology of religion for scholars and students of both religion and psychology. Certainly, there were grounds for discussion, argument, and dispute, but that the two fields of study had been brought to a creative synthesis of methodological insights and analysis would not again be seriously disputed by either religionists or psychologists.

The creation of a term, however, is not synonymous with the creation of a scholarly discipline of study. E(dwin) D(iller) Starbuck (1866-1947) was quite clearly aware of that but was, nevertheless, intent upon launching an enquiry with wide sweeping implications for both the discipline of psychology and the general field of religious studies. He did this with countless articles published in the best peer-reviewed journals but his book, *The Psychology of Religion,* published in New York in 1899 by Charles Scribner's proved to be the stone that truly rippled the scholarly waters for it was Starbuck who was the very first to use the actual term "psychology of religion." An Indiana Quaker and a sequential product of Indiana University (B.A.), Harvard University (M.A.) and Clark University (Ph.D.), Starbuck's major influences were William James at Harvard and G. Stanley Hall at Clark. The impetus for his pursuit of the psychology of religion as a lifelong field of study came from F. Max Muller's 1890 classic, *Introduction to the Science of Religion.* Starbuck stayed on at Clark as a research fellow where he worked closely with James H. Leuba (more about whom later). It was during these pivotal years of work that he wrote and published his classic, *The Psychology of Religion,* which went through three editions and was translated into German. Tension with Hall, if not outright jealously on Hall's part, led Starbuck to move on in both his teaching subjects to include philosophy and education and to a series of university venues including the State University of Iowa and the University of Southern California. It was William James who elevated Starbuck to a national figure by using Starbuck's empirical data in James' own book which constitutes the formal beginning of our consideration here. "If one attempts an evaluation of Starbuck's work from the perspective of several generations," says Beit-Hallahmi, 1974: 86), "one might conclude that it will be remembered more by historians of the field than by practitioners. His work may belong with the classics of the field, but it must be numbered with the unread classics, even among scholars." It was not until a quarter of a century after Starbuck's now classic book, *The Psychology of Religion* (1899), and a year before Freud's pivotal *The Future of an Illusion* (1927), that the Hartford Seminary Foundation in Connecticut hosted a conference entitled, "The Possible Contributions of Modern Psychology to the Theory and Practice of Religion" in October of 1926 (Beit-Hallahmi 1974:86).

Historians of the behavioral science would all more or less agree that the two volume study published in 1890, *The Principles of Psychology,* by William James constituted one of the most important events in the history of the emerging science of psychology in this country and, some would argue, throughout the European world as well (Richardson 2006:127). Granted the central place of this work by James in the science of psychology, it is the consensus of both psychologists and religionists that his *The Varieties of Religious Experience,* published in 1902, constituted the formal beginnings of the emergence of the sub-field of study in both psychology and religion now established as the psychology of religion. William James (1842-1910) was born into wealth, elegance, and eccentricity, being the son of a Swedenborgian theologian, Henry James, Sr., and the older brother of the subsequently internationally acclaimed novelists, Henry James. The godson of Ralph Waldo Emerson, William James attempted a career as an artist but found science, finally, more to his temperament and liking, discovered as a student at the Lawrence Scientific School of Harvard University where he continued as a medical student, taking his M.D. degree from Harvard Medical School in 1869, never, alas, to actually practice medicine (Richardson 2006:149).

With no formal training in psychology *per se*, rather in biology, physiology, and anatomy, he once said that "the first lecture on psychology I ever heard was the first I ever gave" (James 1902:31). Not daunted by this lack of formal training, both James and Harvard pressed on in the creation of an experimental psychology course in 1875 which was attended, over several years, by some of Harvard's subsequently most illustrious students including none other than G. Stanley Hall. Suffering for years from heart problems, James died at his home in New Hampshire on August 29, 1910, holding out to the very end as a functional psychologist and pragmatic philosopher.

It was *The Varieties of Religious Experience* (1902), however, that established him as a proponent of the value and efficacy of religious experience, making him the darling of laymen everywhere and the bane and nemesis of empirical psychologists throughout the English-speaking world. This book, not approaching the scientific value of his *The Principles of Psychology* (1890), netted him the invitation from the University of Edinburgh to give the 1901 and 1902 Gifford Lectures, a forum wherein he was at liberty to chide the scientific community for its dismissive attitude toward the "value" of religious experience in deference to the "origins and ideas of religion." This criticism took the psychological investigation of religious phenomena into a whole new realm of viability and possibility, for, as Charles Pearce is reported to have said, "James has penetrated into the hearts of people" with his sympathetic approach to the "value of religious experience." Yet, his friend and colleague, George Santayana, responding with a resounding scientific critique of James' work by pointing out that the "great weakness of his (James') position is its tendency to disintegrate the idea of truth" in deference to "belief without reason" (Page 1951:4-5).

Just over a dozen years after the publication of James' Gifford Lectures, J. H. Leuba published the book that would take James' work into a whole new and higher dimension of scientific respectability within the psychological community. Leuba's book, *Psychological Origin and Nature of Religion* (London: Constable and Company, 1915), constituted a culmination of countless minor and esoteric studies of various religious phenomenon by a plethora of psychologists, most being former students of both James and G. Stanley Hall at Harvard, Leuba (1868-1948) being among the most prolific researchers and writers in the field. A Swiss by birth and early education, Leuba studied under G. Stanley Hall at Clark University where he graduated in 1895 and he stayed on as a research fellow until moving to Bryn Mawr College to become head of the psychology department (Leuba 1896).

A prolific researcher and writer, he eventually participated in the 1926 International Congress of Psychology in Germany in which he contributed a paper on a panel he shared with Ernest Jones (Leuba 1926b:729). Of major significance was that fact that Leuba was consistently a student and faculty colleagues of E. D. Starbuck, both at Clark under G. Stanley Hall, and at Harvard under William James. The two, Starbuck and Leuba, worked closely together throughout their careers and it was only coincidence that Starbuck, rather than Leuba, actually coined the term "psychology of religion" for they both were early and major players in its development. Besides his major books (1915; 1926a), Leuba's significant contribution to the advancement of the study of psychology of religion as a scientific researcher came when he presented a paper at the Hartford Seminary Foundation's 1926 congress on "the possible contributions of modern psychology to the theory and practice of religion," (Leuba 1926a) a gathering of scholars which included Starbuck and Hall as well. Unlike James' work, which argued for the "value of religion" without attempting an assessment as to its etiology, Leuba brought to bear all of the available analytical tools of scientific enquiry into the meaning and nature of human behavioral responses to perceived and experienced encounter with what was thought, by the subject, to be of a "religious" nature. Here was the application of the psychological science of behavior gone well beyond James' sympathetic and empathetic embrace of the *sui generis* character of religious experience. From Leuba onward, the psychology of religion focused upon the empirical evidence of behavior and the *Psychological Origin and Nature of Religion* (1915) took its place at the head of the class.

No case needs to be made for the lofty ranking of Sigmund Freud in the study of either psychology or religion, for whether one is in favor of his system of thought or not, no one would be so irresponsible as to deny his primacy in such discussions as these. Whether early in his career writing *Totem and Taboo* (1918) or late in his career writing *Moses and Monotheism* (1939), Freud was always there and ready to contribute to and critique any serious discussion of religious behavior. An Austrian born neurologist driven by a desire to break from the oppression of anti-Semitism among his colleagues and to establish himself as a pioneer in medical research, Freud (1856 - 1939) set out to establish a school of thought and enquiry and he succeeded far beyond his greatest expectations. After finishing medical school and studying with some of the great minds of the day including the Parisian Jean Martin Charcot, he set up on his own a psychiatric practice in his home town of Vienna and eventually establish a system of analysis and treatment, viz., psychoanalysis, which was to sweep Europe and America with such profundity and comprehensiveness that, even today, it is impossible to think of social criticism, counseling psychology, or psychiatric practice without having to deal with Freudian theory (Gay 1988:7). At the end of his life, Freud and psychoanalysis were household words and professional juggernauts in the world of psychiatry and psychotherapy. And, to be honest about it, they both still are.

Between *Totem and Taboo* and *Moses and Monotheism* however, Freud wrote a little book, *The Future of an Illusion* (1927) which, without question, placed him front and center in all current and future discussions of the psychology of religion. If his *Civilization and Its Discontents* (1930) is one of the great 20th century critiques of western civilization, then his book on the future of an illusion is comparably one of the greatest criticisms of popularly practiced religion in western civilization. From William James, who wished to emphasize the "value" of religious experience whether or not the experience is real and true, to Leuba, who wished to emphasize the analytical requirement of a scientific methodology in studying experience described as religious behavior, the psychology of religion took a giant leap into respectability. With Freud, empowered by this liberated spirit of scientific enquiry into religious experience and behavior itself, he was able to employ his psychoanalytic methodology without restraint. Proposing that society is established upon the fundamental renunciation of instinct, Freud contends that religion is simultaneously an "instrument of coercion" and a "compensation for the stifled desires of mankind." Religion, he argues, functions as a substitute for the repressed desires which cannot be satisfied due to social restrictions on instinctual human behavior.

Freud is quick, even eager, to identify the benefits of the socialization of the human animal through the cultivation of culture including our moral development, our artistic and ideological refinements, and even our religious systems, illusory though they prove to be. Particularly with religion, Freud, as a psychoanalyst and social critic, is keen to draw poignant attention to the functions and values of religion to society and to the inevitable future of these functions and values as mechanisms of sublimation and repression of our natural instincts. Granted, religion provides a worldview and ethos of explanation as to the verities of life -- where we come from, who we are, where we are going -- but, says Freud, all of these function to stifle and inhibit natural aspirations which are contradictory to the needs and interests of society. Religion, then, provides an optional substitute for our desires which is socially acceptable. But the price is great. In exchange for an All-Seeing God, a father-imago, who looks over us and sees after us, humanity relinquishes our right to pursue our own fulfillment as individuals, ever stifled and inhibited by the rules laid down by the Overseer. The conflict between the individual and society is matched and surpassed by the conflict between individual desires and the constraints derived and administered by God. Religion is humanity's formalized response to our own feelings of insecurity, incompetence, and lack of control over the environment. The only genuine solution, says Freud, is for humanity to throw off this illusory source of an All Powerful God and assert our own independence with all of the dangers and risks implied by doing so.

From James to Leuba to Freud is no simple nor easy jump, but once it was made, there was no turning back. Freud demonstrated both the destructive and constructive power of psychological analysis of religious ideology and behavior. Whether one agreed with his psychoanalytic assessment, and many did not then nor do they now, nevertheless, the astuteness and acuteness of his analysis and critique set the psychological and religious world on its heels and what followed proved to be provocative and creative in the scholarly world. However, it took Carl Gustav Jung (1875-1961) of Zurich to recapture the religious world's interest in depth psychology's analysis of religion after the devastating blow from Freud. Jung was an avoid, though somewhat and sometimes less than traditionally orthodox, Christian and the son of a Swiss Reformed Church pastor. Though early on he was attracted to and influenced by Freud and psychoanalysis, Jung subsequently branched out on his own "and that has made all the difference." He took his medical degree from the University of Basel and launched his professional career in the Burgholzli, a psychiatric hospital in Zurich, alongside none other than Eugene Bleuler, a colleague who was early own to prove to be an important confidant and collaborator. Following a period of close collegiality with Freud, during which time Freud anticipated Jung becoming his protégé, Jung broke with him over issues related to infantile sexuality and dream interpretation. As prolific a writer as Freud himself, Jung's career as a therapist was paralleled by his career as a writer, and though his book, *Psychology of the Unconscious* (1912) launched him into international notoriety, his little book, *Psychology and Religion,* based on the Terry Lectures given at Yale University in 1938, undoubtedly established him as a major player in the psychological study of religion, competing with Freud and psychoanalysis as the major school of depth psychology.

Unlike Freud, who seemed to have a personal agenda regarding the negative influences of religion on human freedom and personal development, Jung came with a positive assessment of the phenomenon, albeit somewhat unorthodox in his characterization of the impetus and motivation for the religious life. In 1952, during his declining years as a now popular sage, he wrote: "I find that all my thoughts circle around God like the planets around the sun, and are as irresistibly attracted by Him. I would feel it to be the grossest sin if I were to oppose any resistance to this force" (1963:xi). It is only here in his autobiography that Jung ever spoke of his personal relationship to God, choosing rather, as in his Terry Lectures, to maintain a professional distance and what he considered to be a scientifically respectable posture. "Notwithstanding the fact that I have often been called a philosopher, I am an empiricist and adhere to the phenomenological standpoint" he said in his opening remarks in the Terry Lectures at Yale University (1938:1).

Jung, differing radically from Freud on this analytical point, argued that the increase in western society of the scientific understanding of the world has led us into a dehumanization of the natural and social environments in which we live and, thus, our prehistoric and primitive responsiveness to occurrences in the natural world have lost their "symbolic efficacy." Therefore, he suggested, modern man has lost touch, has become alienated, from his natural environment. This loss, contended Jung, has led humanity away from a belief in God and has produced a lack of awareness of powers implicit within human nature. Modern society has, therefore, fallen into the grip of psychological disorder and chaos. We are in desperate need, says Jung, of a religious mooring, a religiously-based worldview and ethos, to re-align ourselves with the "collective unconscious" which infuses all of our conscious and unconscious thoughts, actions, and dreams. While religion cannot be proven either true or false, it is quite apparent that the pragmatic value of religious ideology and its resulting belief system served the psychological needs of man "in search of his soul" (Jung 1933:12) While contending vociferously for the universality of the collective unconscious, Jung is quick to point out that there is no possibility of empirically verifying its reality other than in the effectiveness of its use in the treatment of psychological disorders. "At the root of the problem," says Edward (1967:389), "lies an ambiguous set of ontological claims. ... it is worth noting that we possess no statistical evidence of a worthwhile kind about the efficacy of Jungian psychotherapy." Be that as it may, the acclaim Jung's Terry Lectures received particularly from the religious establishment and theological community of the time was profoundly instrumental in placing Jungian psychology front and center in the development of what would eventuate into a pastoral psychology embraced by virtually every seminary in the country.

By the middle of the 20th century, the touchstones of the development of the psychology of religion as a *bona fide,* however yet fledgling, discipline of study, though many had contributed, were clearly the pivotal works of James, Leuba, Freud, and Jung. From respectable curiosity to depth analysis, the "psychological" nature of religious ideology and behavior was well established, thanks to these four individuals who were, of course, buttressed by the works of many, though lesser, researcher and writers of the time (Beit-Hallahmi 1974; Henry 1938; page 1951; Schaud 1923; Schaud 1924; Strunk 1957). And, though Jung was unabashed in his allegiance to Christianity, being the son of a Christian minister and himself a psychiatrist who did not fail to traffic in Christianity nomenclature, nevertheless, a full fledged address to the relationship between the Christian view of the human condition and the relevance of a scientific psychology had not yet occurred. All of that changed profoundly in 1950 with the publication of *Psychotherapy and a Christian View of Man* by David E. Roberts of Union Theological Seminary in New York City. That same year, three leading psychologists would publish their contributions to the field of psychology of religion and, with these four books, the discipline of psychology of religion was well positioned to claim a rightful place at the table in both academies of psychology and religious studies.

David E. Roberts (1911 - 1955) was an Omaha, Nebraska, native and the son of the Rev. Dr. William E. Roberts. He graduated in 1931 from Occidental College and went on to earn his Bachelor of Divinity *maga cum laude* from the Union Theological Seminary in New York City. Having earned a traveling fellowship from the Seminary, he traveled and studied extensively in Germany and England, earning his Ph.D. from the University of Edinburgh in Scotland, and returning to the Seminary in 1936 as a member of the faculty, first as instructor, and then in rapid succession assistant professor, associate professor, the Marcellus Hartley Professor of the Philosophy of Religion and Dean of Students by 1950, dying in his sleep at the early age of 44 in 1955. A Phi Beta Kappa and prolific writer of scholarly articles for the leading journals of the day, his only book was the now classic and at the time internationally acclaimed *Psychotherapy and a Christian View of Man,* published in New York by Charles Scriber's Sons in 1950. A brief 161 page study, it was poised to change the face of psychological studies of Christian thought in every major seminary in the United States. Both Rollo May, a leading psychotherapist of the time, and Paul Tillich, the leading liberal Protestant theologian of the 20th century, joined in touting the originality of Roberts' study and Seward Hiltner of Princeton, the leading authority in the fledgling field at the time of pastoral care and counseling, mandated that all pastors and theologians as well as psychologists and psychotherapists owed it to themselves and their profession to become acquainted with "this remarkable book."

Roberts' work was cut out for him in this study because, on the one hand, he had to tread lightly, but confidently, amidst the psychological nomenclature and analysis of religious behavior, satisfying both psychiatry and secular psychologists, while simultaneously threading his way through the theological maze of fundamental Christian concepts such as creation, the Fall, sin, grace, predestination, and salvation. To please the medical and psychological community was ominous, but to complicate that by attempting to at least stay clear of major battles with divergent theologies within the Christian camp was quite another. He did it with aplomb to, seemingly, the satisfaction and commendation of both disciplines of psychology and theology.

Granted that Roberts' theocentricism and, sometimes quite conspicuously, his christocenticism took a major hand in setting the agenda for discussion of the interrelatedness of psychotherapy (and its seasoned partner psychoanalysis) and Christian theology, nevertheless, he is eager to demonstrate that a mature theological methodology would and should incorporate psychological components in its concept of the human person. Sin and depression, therapy and forgiveness, salvation and wholeness constitute parallels in psychology and religion and his attempt was to demonstrate how both professions can work together for the benefit of the individual without necessarily relinquishing the unique domain of each. Whether he succeeded or not is not so important for us here as to realize that the discipline of the psychology of religion took a major stride forward in fostering dialogue between the two disciplines and the two professions of clergy and psychologists in a way that all previous attempts had neither tried nor succeeded. To even place the terms "psychotherapy" and "Christian" within the same title of the book was monumental and set the stage for the next twenty-five years of dialogue between the professions.

Though Roberts was responsible for bringing depth psychology and Christianity theology into direct dialogue, the psychology of religion was not destined to morph into a sub-set of Christian thought. The pursuit of the role and application of the psychology of religion was from the beginning perceived to be more broadly cast. Later in the century, we will see psychology of religion focus again upon specific religious traditions with Bakan on Judaism and Homans and Erikson on Christianity. But for now, it fell to Gordon Willard Allport (1897-1967) to refocus upon the interfacing of psychology and religion. The son of a country doctor from Montezuma, Indiana, and the product of an iconic exemplification of the Protestant religion and work ethic, Allport, along with his mother and their numerous children, assisted the father in a family-run hospital and clinic. Following his older brothers to Harvard University, Allport took his B.A., M.A., and Ph.D.(1922) and, winning a coveted traveling fellowship, spent two years studying at, first, the Gestalt School in Berlin, Germany, and another year at Cambridge University in England. First taking a teaching position in psychology at Harvard University, he then taught for four years at Dartmouth College before returning to spend the remainder of his academic career back at Harvard. Becoming the editor of the *Journal of Abnormal and Social Psychology,* Allport went on to be President of the American Psychological Association and President of the Society for the Psychological Study of Social Issues, dying in Cambridge, MA, at the age of seventy years old.

Allport's internationally acclaimed study of the nature of personal religion in the development of the individual, *The Individual and His Religion*, was published by Macmillan in 1950, and became a recognized classic in the study of the function of religious sentiment in the personality of the individual. Five years later, his *Becoming: Basic Considerations for a Psychology of Personality* (1955)would clench his reputation. Neither a Freudian nor a Jungian, but rather falling loosely into the social psychology school of the time, Allport did quote Jung in saying that, of his thousands of patients over the age of thirty-five with which he dealt, "all have been people whose problem in the last resort was that of finding a religious outlook on life (Jung,1933)." Allport's interest was the relationship between religious beliefs and practices -- ideology and behavior -- as relates to the maturation process of the personality, contending that religion in an individual's life can mature along with his or her personality if attended to properly. Yet, he never argued for the truthfulness of religion, merely its influence upon individual maturation, both for good and ill. "My effort," he wrote in the Preface of this little classic, "is directed solely to a portrayal of the place of subjective religion in the structure of personality whenever and wherever religion has such a place. My approach is psychological ... I make no assumptions and no denials regarding the claims of revealed religion" (1950:xi). Here was a recognized psychologist from an established school applying his science to the study of religious ideology and behavior. It was internationally acclaimed and set the bar even higher for both disciplines in that, irrespective of the truthfulness of religious belief, there is indisputably a "relationship" between what one believes about the meaning and purpose of his or her individual life and the development and maturity of that individual's personality and well-being. Allport said of his work: "A man's religion is the audacious bid he makes to bind himself to creation and to the Creator. It is his ultimate attempt to enlarge and to complete his own personality by finding the supreme context in which he rightly belongs. In these pages, I have undertaken the task of discovering the place of religion in the life-economy of the individual, of seeking a psychological understanding of the nature and functioning of the religious sentiment, and tracing the full course of religious development in the normally mature and productive personality" (1950:9). This he did and, setting the bar higher than yet having been set, he challenged scholars and researchers in both camps, psychology and religion, to demonstrate the viability and efficacy of this interfacing agenda.

Eric Fromm (1900-1980), A German psychoanalyst and the only child of Orthodox Jewish parents, was educated at the University of Frankfurt am Main in jurisprudence before transferring to the University of Heidelberg where he studied sociology under Max Weber's younger brother, Alfred, as well as psychiatry under Karl Jaspers. Taking his Ph.D. in sociology from Heidelberg in 1922, he went on to become a psychoanalyst at the Frieda Reichmann's psychoanalytic sanatorium in Heidelberg after which he joined the Frankfurt Institute for Social Research where he completed his training and residency. Fleeing Nazi Germany in the 1930s, he went to Geneva and subsequently to New York where he taught at the New School for Social Research and then at Columbia University where he became a life-long colleague and confidant of Karen Horney whose book, *Self Analysis* (1942), reflects their close association in life and thought. Working in the development of the New York Branch of the Washington School of Psychiatry after leaving Columbia, Fromm became a co-founder of the William Alanson White Institute of Psychiatry, Psychoanalysis, and Psychology. He later moved to Mexico City and taught on the National Autonomous University faculty in the medical school before returning to teach psychology at Michigan State University and, subsequently, at New York University. He died in his home in Switzerland at the age of eighty years old, all the while maintaining an active clinical practice.

Whereas Allport, as a social psychologist whose international notoriety was set by his 1941 *Escape from Freedom*, brought the study of the psychology of religion to focus upon the value and function of religious ideology for the individual, whether religion was true or not, Fromm, as a psychoanalyst, chose to emphasize the efficacy of psychoanalytic insights into the human condition which religion serves. Religion is not in danger of scientific scrutiny nor is psychoanalysis treading on forbidden ground. Rather, whereas religion addresses a fundamental need found in the human condition, psychoanalysis provides a scientific mechanism to understand, assess, and facilitate an address to that human situation, a condition which is fraught with fear, anxiety, and uncertainty about the verities of life and our future in it. "Psychoanalysis assesses the persistent tension between traditional religion and the underlying philosophy of psychoanalysis," explains Fromm, "which many believe regards the satisfaction of instinctive and material wishes as the sole aim of life." Fromm argues that "psychoanalysis is neither the enemy of religion nor its ally but rather is concerned with the human reality behind theological doctrines and with the realization of the human values underlying all great religious teachings" (Fromm 1950). Though his 1956 classic, *The Art of Loving*, is considered his greatest work, catapulting him into international notoriety as a psychoanalytically insightful social critique, it was his inquiry into the nature and function of religious belief and practice and its relationship to the healthy, inquisitive, and scientifically astute human mind, namely, *Psychoanalysis and Religion* (1950), which proved to be just that approach to the psychology of religion which made it equally and legitimately the domain of both psychologists and theologians alike.

The profundity of the psychoanalytic school founded by Sigmund Freud was clouded by the wake of great practitioners who, because of its inordinately imperialistic claim to exclusivity in psychotherapeutic theory and practice. As Alfred Adler and Carl Jung fell by the wayside into professional censorship from Freud and his society of practitioners, so, likewise, did Otto Rank (1884-1939). This, however, was profoundly surprising as Rank was perceived by the inner circle to be "Freud's heir apparent" and certainly his "right-hand man." Rank, an Austrian-born psychoanalysis and a medical graduate of the University of Vienna, chose rather than to focus upon the more commonly accepted clinical application of psychoanalytic practice to address issues implicit in mythology, literature, religion, and the arts, a decision which seemed to have pleased Freud initially a great deal. His first major work, which gained Freud acclamation, was his *Art and Artist* (1907) which employed Freud's theory of dream mechanisms to explain the mental processes operative within the artist's mind. A founder of the International Psychoanalytical Association and its Secretary for a number of years, after a falling out with Freud over Rank's unwillingness to continue to tout the Oedipus Complex as the center piece of his own emerging psychoanalytic theory of human motivation as reflected in Rank's 1924 book, *The Trauma of Birth*, Freud removed him from both the editorship of the *Internationale Zeitschrift fur Psychoanalyse* and membership in the IPA. Consequently, Rank left Vienna with his wife and daughter and moved his prestigious psychoanalytic practice to Paris where he remained busy as both a practitioner and research/writer for much of the remainder of his life, moving finally to New York City where he died in 1939, just five weeks after the death of Freud.

The courage to break from Freud was epic and iconic on Rank's part, having been designated publicly by Freud as his successor to the leadership of the psychoanalytic movement within psychiatry. But for Rank to address the taboo topic of "the soul" was nothing short of monumental. Yet, Rank's interest on the relationship between the discipline of psychology and the human experience he calls "the soul" was pivotal in his own development. The human will to live forever against death, the conflict between the individual and social consciousness which has produced both "consolation and inspiration" is what Rank came to call the "immortal soul," and he chose unabashedly to introduce the concept within the developing discipline of psychology of religion. "Dealing with life, experience, growth, the soul, and man's need to believe in immortality, this volume (says the publisher) provides a penetrating study of man's spiritual development through the ages, of man's efforts to sustain himself spiritually in the face of knowledge and doubt, and of his destructive and creative strivings to come to terms with death" (1950:ix). The book's central thesis is that intellectual psychology cannot give the human person the immortal soul deserves, and that the consolation of attempting to rationalize spiritual matters out of existence, which too many psychologists have offered their followers, is futile. We must face reality, says Rank, no mater how painful it may be. Courage, to be sure, was the force behind Rank's challenge to psychology to confront honesty and boldly the reality of the soul and for theologians, without pride or condescension, to realize the profound insight psychology offers to an understanding of the driving forces within the human spirit. Beyond Allport, who wanted us to accept the function of religion, whether true or not, Rank wants us to accept the truth of the human quest for immortality against the inevitabilities of death and the key role that religion plays in that quest.

Near the end of the decade of the 1950s which, as we have noted, include blockbuster studies in the psychology of religion by Roberts, Allport, Fromm, and Rank, David Bakan (1921-2004), an adventurous psychologist who had taken his Ph.D. (1948) at Ohio State University and fresh to the University of Chicago (1961-1968) by way of the University of Missouri (1949-1961), came onto the scene with a radical application of etiological sleuthing applied to Sigmund Freud. A prolific writer and one whose courage matched that of Otto Rank's in daring to revisit the ideological infrastructure of Freud's psychoanalytic theories themselves, Bakan wrote the book for psychologists that equaled the insightfulness of Roberts' work written for Christian clergy. Ending his long and distinguished career at York University in Toronto where he died in 2004, Bakan had been an executive member of the American Psychological Association and on the Advisory Board of the Canadian Council on Children and Youth. One of his international distinctions was his becoming the founding editor of the *Canadian Journal of Community Mental Health.*

Bakan's *Sigmund Freud and the Jewish Mystical Tradition* published, in 1958 by D.Van Nostrand Company of Princeton, New Jersey, was destined, from day one, to become a controversial classic in the field of the history of psychoanalysis and a pillar of support for the psychology of religion. Bakan goes on to have a distinguished career as a scholar and teacher at York University in Canada, but this book, which came out upon his arrival at the University of Chicago, established him as a pivotal player in this emerging disciplinc. In the second edition, published by Schocken Books of New York, the publisher points out that Bakan chose to accept Freud's own distinction between being a Jew and his acceptance of Jewish doctrine and, by using this distinction as a hermeneutical tool, "demonstrates what power Jewish mystical doctrine retained in the formation of Freud's technical genius" (1958:ix). This had not been attempted, even hinted at, prior to Bakan and the boldness of the venture elevated the psychology of religion as a field of study to that of a national agenda. "By sharpening the reader's perspective about the ways in which Freud was, and was not, Jewish," says Schocken, Bakan presented a book that spoke to the fate of all people in the modern world, an inquiry into the nature of the relationship between the etiology of faith and the development of the human personality. It set the stage for the next fifty years of research in the psychology of religion as regards the relationship between religious ideology and religious behavior.

What Bakan did to Freud, Erik Erikson (1902-1994) did to Martin Luther, the father of the Protestant Reformation. Erikson's (1958) *Young Man Luther: A Study in Psychoanalysis and History,* published by W. W. Norton and Company of New York, came off the press, without orchestration of collaboration, the same year Bakan's book on Freud was released. Called "a very profound study" by none other than Reinhold Neibuhr of Harvard, the book demonstrated the deep insights into theological speculation the etiology of psychological development can offer. As with Bakan on Freud, Erikson on Luther produced a whirlwind of acclaim and controversy.

Erik Erikson (known during his childhood and early adulthood as Erik Homburger owing to a complicated history of patrimony) was the son of a prominent Jewish mother from Copenhagen and he was raised in the Jewish faith. Born in Frankfurt, Germany, he studied in Vienna with Anna Freud and become a trained psychoanalyst at the Vienna Psychoanalytic Institute as well as a teacher from the Montessori Academy there. Never receiving any university degree, these two experiences were his only documented training credentials but he went on, following immigration with his wife, to Boston where he set up as the first child psychoanalyst in that city, taking positions at the Massachusetts General Hospital as well as the Harvard Medical School's Psychological Clinic. Never one to question his own talents and abilities, he pushed forward in Boston and at Harvard, eventually landing an appointment at Yale University's Human Relations Institute and Medical School, all the while honing his skills as a clinician, researcher, and writer. He eventually took a post at the Institute of Child Welfare at the University of California at Berkeley during which time he wrote the book that made him famous, *Childhood and Society* (1950), which subsequently went through numerous revisions and editions. Leaving California, he went to teach at the Austen Riggs Center, a prominent psychiatric treatment facility in Stockbridge, MA, but subsequently returned to Harvard as Professor of Human Development where he remained until his death in 1994.

"Identify crisis" is one of many terms created by Erikson in developing his eight stages of development, moving beyond and above the standard five stages developed by the father of psychoanalysis himself, Sigmund Freud. Erikson, always eager to best his betters, his eight stages catapulted him into stardom, a reputation he protected even to the extent of failing to acknowledge that one of his sons was institutionalized from infancy in a sanitarium in California due to Down Syndrome, not even attending the young man's funeral and only telling his other children of Neil's existence at the time of his death. The image of the perfect family was crucial to Erikson, the father of developmental psychology, and, thus, Neil was pushed into oblivion.

Erikson's work on Luther, *Young Man Luther: A Study in Psychoanalysis and History.* N.Y.: W. W. Norton, 1958, was nothing short of brilliant. Moving psychology of religion beyond merely a dialogic encounter between psychologists and theologians, Erikson chose the biography of one of the greatest religious leaders in western Christian history as the focus of his psychoanalytic attention. And, to be sure, it proved epic in its implications and ramifications. Erikson's own personal history, the contrast between who he really was and who he thought he was growing up (owing to complications of marital impropriety and a failure of discretion), led him to identify with Luther's own personal identify crisis, the struggle between what the Church said it was and what it proved to be in Luther's experience. Therein lay the nexus for a psychoanalytic story worth the telling. Erikson told it with insight, provocation, and creativity. And when it was told, both the psychological community and the Christian community were ready to do battle over issues related to psychological development and faith experience. The book was a profoundly telling insight into the biography of a religious leader, from his initial doubts to his final commitments and the book has proven a great tool for pastoral psychology and counseling in dealing with religious etiology of behavioral crises.

With Bakan's analysis of Freud and Erikson's analysis of Luther having precipitated a raging national debate, the stage was set for a frontal attack upon the institution of religion itself, an attack which simultaneously condemned the institutionalization of religion while affirming the efficacy of the religious experience. That task was eagerly embraced by Abraham Harold Maslow (1908 - 1970). Maslow was born in Brooklyn, New York, the first of seven children to parents who were uneducated Jews from Russia. Because he was intellectually gifted, he distinguished himself at the Brooklyn Borough High School. His father's ambition for him to study law lasted only a few weeks at the City College of New York and, after transferring to Cornell for a few courses, Maslow returned to CCNY but failed to complete his degree. Maslow married his high school sweetheart when he was 20 and his bride 19. He, then, applied to and was accepted at the University of Wisconsin where he earned his B.A. in 1930, his M.A. in 1931, and his Ph.D. in 1934, all in psychology. After serving on the Wisconsin faculty as Assistant Instructor in Psychology (1930-1934) and Teaching Fellow in Psychology (1934-1935), Maslow was back to New York to Teacher's College, Columbia University, where he became interested specifically in research on human sexuality. At Columbia, he served as a Carnegie Fellow from 1935-1937. Unlike Freud, Jung, and Adler, Maslow was disinclined to focus his attention and research upon the mentally ill, preferring to study why and how people are mentally healthy, happy, and fulfilled. Eventually, he would develop a whole psychodynamic schema of theoretical constructs and a conceptual framework called the "hierarchy of needs." From 1951 to 1969, he taught at Brandeis University where he developed the concept of "self-actualization." Maslow was elected president of the American Psychological Association and became the founding editor of both the *Journal of Humanistic Psychology* and the *Journal of Transpersonal Psychology*. The recognized head of what became known as the Third Force in psychology, that is, the humanistic school *vis a vis* Freudian psychology and behaviorism, Maslow ended his teaching carrier as the first Resident Fellow of the W. P. Laughlin Charitable Foundation in Menlo Park where he died on the 8th of June, 1970, at the age of sixty-two.

Not religion itself but the institutionalization of religion, rather than the experience and value of religious sentiment, was the victim of Maslow systematic dissection. Maslow contended unabashedly that "man has a higher and transcendent nature, and," he pointed out, "this is part of his essence," even suggesting that it is actually part of his biological nature as a member of a species which has evolved through history. The book which made it all come together was his 1970 *Religions, Values, and Peak-Experiences* published by Penguin of New York. Maslow's criticism suggested that the institutionalization of religious experience had cost the individual severely. An instant best seller, Maslow's opening statement se the tone for the whole book: "Organized Religion, the churches, finally may become the major enemies of the religious experience and the religious experiencer. This is a main thesis of this book" (1970:4). Whereas David Roberts had attempted to show

how psychotherapy and Christian theology could compliment each other and Allport had argued for the "value" of religious experience, whether true or not, and whereas Bakan had shown the influence of Hassidic mysticism upon the theories of Freud's psychoanalysis while Erkison demonstrated the value of a psychoanalytic analysis of a religious fanatic like Luther, Maslow was the first of the leading psychologists to frontally attack "organized religion" itself, and he did it by simultaneously affirming and vindicating the meaning and value of the religious experience is valid and true for the individual. This was transformative in the field of psychology for now the science was able to demonstrate a capacity at social criticism without posturing as an "atheistic" endeavor to dislodge religion from the individual. Rather, it was a demonstration of how the institutions of religion could meaningfully and effectively be dislodged from the authentic religious experience itself. This Maslow did in his *Religions, Values, and Peak-Experiences,* thereby empowering both the science of psychology to proceed with its analytical agenda as well as validating and authenticating members of society who thought of themselves as "spiritual" without being "religious." His two previous books, *Toward a Psychology of Being* (1962) and *The Psychology of Science: A Reconnaissance* (1966) set the scholarly standard for the writing of the book on religious values. His final work, *The Farter Reaches of Human Nature* (1971) assured Maslow of a place in the history of psychology. Today, the whole secular spirituality movement of individuals who seek to affirm and nurture their feelings of spirituality while denying any attraction to or subjectivity to religious institutions. Spirituality without the church, synagogue, or mosque was what came out of Maslow's analysis and that sentiment still persists throughout modern western society today.

The consensus among the respondents from the

eighteen theological schools approached in preparation for this article is that Peter Homans' 1970 *Theology After Freud,* published by Bobbs-Merrill, constitutes the culminating work which set in place the discipline of the psychology of religion. Gerald Gargiulo said it best in his review of the book: "What happens to theology *after* it allows itself to experience Freud is the theme of the work" (1971:99). For the first time, the discipline of theology itself, i.e., the methodological approach to the study of God by people of faith, was challenged to encounter a psychoanalytic school of thought. The effort was not to try and understand the individual's religious experience but rather to bring face to face the two disciplines, their methodologies, domain assumptions, operational modalities of analysis and expostulations. Theology encountering psychology and *vise versa* was what Homans called for and did. This was pivotal and monumental and both disciplines were called to arms and, more importantly, challenged to be fair and responsive to the other.

Peter Humans (1930-2009) was a native of New York City and graduated from Princeton University, earning his divinity degree from the Virginia Theological Seminary and an M.A. and Ph.D. from the Divinity School of the University of Chicago in 1964. He taught social science and the history of religion at the University of Chicago from 1965 to 2001, when he retired. At the time of his death, the Dean of the Divinity School, Rick Rosengarten, said of Homans: "For over three decades, Peter Homans was a distinguished teacher and advisor to students at the Divinity School and in the University, and a leading thinker about psychology as a -- if not the -- decisive cultural expression of the 20th century."

Beginning with an assessment of the viability and utility of William James' study of the wide range and depth of religious experiences, Homans sought a possible reinterpretation of the theological terms "transcendence" and "immanence" within the context of what he called a "third reading of Freud." Using Reinhold Niebuhr and Paul Tillich as representatives of classic existential theology, he faced off with his third reading, namely, an "iconic reading" *vis a vis* "mechanistic" and "dynamic" readings, and suggested a theology of nostalgia be perceived as immanence and hope as transcendence. Though there is serious dispute among psychoanalysts with his attempted "redefinition" of theological terms using a psychoanalytic license which some question his right to use, Homans proceeded, however, to call to task Christian theologians on precisely this point of definitional nomenclature, calling them to explore and employ more contemporary and scientifically viable terms for the transcendent and immanent experience within religious experience. "Christian thought, for the most part," he said, "has been a theology without a psychology, and Christian man has regularly decided to understand his psychology, when he wanted it at all, under the control of his theology." Homans then concluded his preface by saying that, therefore, "the purpose of this book, then, is to explicate the issues and lines of relation between these three foci: the way that theology, in defining itself, distinguishes itself from psychoanalysis, the possibility of different understandings of psychoanalysis that such a distinction raises; and the part psychoanalysis has to play in what theologians and others call the process of secularization" (1970:12). Whether he pulled it off or not is not our concern here. Rather, we wish to emphasize that as Homans began with an analysis of William James in his approach to Freud and psychoanalysis in pursuit of a theological understanding of religious experience, he brought the discipline of the psychology of religion to a level of maturity which heretofore was lacking. His contribution to the establishment of the discipline is indisputable. What the discipline has chosen to do in the last quarter of the 20th century with its legacy calls for a further enquiry.

CONCLUDING COMMENT

From William James to Peter Homans is a seventy-year span of time commencing with a call to investigate religious experience and concluding with a clarion call for theology and psychology to converge upon the phenomenon of religious experience with scientific integrity and theological responsibility. The twelve books considered in this essay are all iconic and epic in the contributions they made to the subjects they covered. That eighteen of the top theological institutions in the United States were asked to collaborate in identifying just what twelve books would be credited with contributing to the development of the discipline of the psychology of religion was, itself, a unique event. It is hoped that the task set before us at the outset has been met and discharged with integrity and credibility.

----

*The eighteen institutions approached were Andover Newton Theological School, Boston University School of Theology, Candler School of Theology (Emory University), Catholic Theological Union, Duke University Divinity School, General Theological Seminary, Graduate Theological Foundation, Harvard University Divinity School, Lutheran School of Theology (Chicago), Perkins School of Theology (Southern Methodist University), Princeton Theological Seminary, San Francisco Theological Seminary, St. John's University School of Theology, St. Joseph's Seminary (New York), Union Theological

Seminary (New York), University of Chicago Divinity School, Yale University Divinity School.

BIBLIOGRAPHY

Allport, Gordon W. (1937) *Personality: A Psychological Interpretation.* N.Y.: Holt.

Allport, Gordon W. (1950) *The Individual and His Religion.* New York: Macmillan.

Allport, Gordon W. (1955) *Becoming: Basic Considerations for a Psychology of Personality.* New Haven, CT: Yale University Press.

Ames, E. S. (1910) *The Psychology of Religious Experience.* Boston: Houghton Mifflin.

Argyle, Michael, and Benjamin Beit-Hallahmi. (1975) *The Social Psychology of Religion.* Boston: Beacon Press.

Bakan, David (1958) *Sigmund Freud and the Jewish Mystical Tradition.* Princeton, NJ: D.Van Nostrand Company.

Beit-Hallahmi, Benjamin (1974). Psychology of Religion, 1880-1930: the Rise and Fall of a Psychological Movement. *Journal of the History of the Behavioral Sciences* 10: 84-90.

Calvin, S. S. (1902) The Psychological Necessity of Religion. *American Journal of Psychology* 15: 10-15.

Coe, G. A. (1916) *The Psychology of Religion.* Chicago: University of Chicago Press.

Edwards, Paul. Editor in Chief. (1967) *The Encyclopedia of Philosophy* Volumes 1-8. New York: Macmillan Publishing Co.

Erikson, Erik (1958) *Young Man Luther: A Study in Psychoanalysis and History.* N.Y.: W. W. Norton and Company.

Erikson, Erik (1962) *Childhood and Society.* New York: W. W. Norton.

Erikson, Erik (1964) *Insight and Responsibility.* New York: W. W. Norton.

Flower, J. C. (1927) *An Approach to the Psychology of Religion.* N.Y.: Harcourt.

Freud, Sigmund (1927 German/ 1953 Vienna) *The Future of an Illusion.* N.Y.: Liveright Publishing Company.

Freud, Sigmund (1939) *Moses and Monotheism.* N.Y.: Vintage Books Edition.

Freud, Sigmund (1930) *Civilization and Its Discontents.* London: Hogarth Press Edition.

Freud, Sigmund (1918) *Totem and Taboo: Resemblances Between the Psychic Lives of Savages and Neurotics* N.Y.: Vintage Books Edition.

Fromm, Eric (1950) *Psychoanalysis and Religion.* New Haven: Yale University Press.

Fromm, Eric ((1941) *Escape from Freedom.* New York: Rinehart & Company.

Fromm, Eric (1956) *The Art of Loving.* New York: Bantam Books.

Fromm, Eric (1973) *The Anatomy of Human Destructiveness.* N.Y.: Rinehart & Winston.

Gargiulo, Gerald J. (1971) Review of Peter Homans' *Theology After Freud* in *American Imago,* Vol. 28, No. 1, 99-103.

Gay, Peter. (1988) *Freud: A Life for Our Time.* N.Y.: W. W. Norton.

Glock, C. Y. and Stark, R. (1965) *Religion and Society in Tension.* Chicago: Rand McNally.

Harre, Rom, and Roger Lamb, Editors (1983) *The Encyclopedic Dictionary of Psychology* (Cambridge, MA: The MIT Press.

Henry, E. R. (1938) A Survey of courses in Psychology Offered by Undergraduate Colleges of Liberal Arts. *Psychological Bulletin* 35:420-435.

Homans, Peter (1970) *Theology After Freud: An Interpretive Inquiry.* Indianapolis: The Bobbs-Merrill Company.

Homans, Peter (1984) *The Ability to Mourn: Disillusionment and the Social Origins of Psychoanalysis.* Chicago: University of Chicago Press.

Horney, Karen (1942) *Self-Analysis.* N.Y.: W. W. Norton.

James, William (1890) *The Principles of Psychology, Volumes 1 and 2.* New York: Holt, Rinehart and Winston.

James, William (1902) *The Varieties of Religious Experience.* N.Y.: Longmans, Green and Company.

Jung, Carl (1938) *Psychology and Religion.* New Haven: Yale University Press.

Jung, Carl (1912) *The Psychology of the Unconscious.* Leipzig: Franz Deuticke.

Jung, Carl (1963) *Memories, Dreams, Reflections.* (London: Collins & Routledge & Kegan Paul.

Jung, Carl (1933) *Modern Man in Search of a Soul* New York: Harcourt, Brace and Company.

Kendler, Howard H. (1987) *Historical Foundations of Modern Psychology* (Chicago, IL: The Dorsey Press).

Leuba, James H. (1896) A Study in the Psychology of Religious Phenomenon. *American Journal of Psychology* 5:309-335.

Leuba, James H. (1915) *Psychological Origin and Nature of Religion.* London: Constable and Company.

Leuba, James H. (1926a) Psychology of Religion. *Psychological Bulletin* 23:714-722.

Leuba, James H. (1926b) Notes on Meetings and Conferences for the Discussion of the Psychology of Religion. *Psychological Bulletin* 23:729.

Maslow, Abraham H. (1970) *Religions, Values, and Peak-Experiences.* N.Y.: Penguin.

Maslow, Abraham H. (1962) *Toward a Psychology of Being.* N.Y.: Van Nostrand.

Maslow, Abraham H. (1966) *The Psychology of Science: A Reconnaisance.* N.Y.: Harper & Row.

Maslow, Abraham H. (1971) *The Farther Reaches of Human Nature.* N.Y.: Viking.

Morgan, John H. (2010) *Beginning With Freud: The Classical Schools of Psychotherapy.* Lima, OH: Wyndham Hall Press.

Morgan, John H. (1987) *From Freud to Frankl: Our Modern Search for Personal Meaning.* (Bristol, IN: Wyndham Hall Press.

Morgan, John H. (2005) *Naturally Good: A Behaviaoral History of Moral Development (from Charles Darwin to E. O. Wilson).* South Bend, IN: Cloverdale Books.

Morgan, John H. (1978) *In Search of Meaning: From Freud to Teilhard de Chardin.* Washington, DC: University Press of America.

Page, F. H. (1951) The Psychology of Religion after Fifty Years. *Canadian Journal of Psychology* 5:60-67.

Pratt, J. B. (1907) *The Psychology of Religious Belief.* N.Y.: Macmillan.

Pratt, J. B. (1905) Psychology of Religion. *Harvard*

Theological Review 1:435-454.

Rank, Otto (1907) *Art and Artist.* N.Y.: W. W. Norton.

Rank, Otto (1924) *The Trauma of Birth.* N.Y.: W. W. Norton.

Rank, Otto (1950 *English Trans.) Psychology and the Soul.* New York: A. S. Barnes & Company.

Reber, Arthur S. (1985) *The Penguin Dictionary of Psychology.* New York: Viking Penguin.

Richardson, Robert D. (2006) *William James: In the Maelstrom of American Modernism.* Boston: Houghton Mifflin.

Rieff, Philip. (1966) *The Triumph of the Therapeutic: Uses of Faith After Freud.* N.Y.: Harper & Row.

Roberts, David E. (1950) *Psychotherapy and A Christian View of Man.* New York: Charles Scribner's.

Schaud, E. L. (1923) The Present Status of the Psychology of Religion. *Journal of Religion* 3:362-379.

Schaud, E. L. (1924) The Psychology of Religion in America during the Past Quarter Century. *Journal of Religion* 4:113-134.

Starbuck, E. D. (1899) *Psychology of Religion.* N.Y.: Scribner's.

Strunk, Oscar. (1957) The Present Status of the Psychology of Religion. *The Journal of Bible and Religion*

John H. Morgan

26:387-392.

CHAPTER NINE
Personal Meaning as Therapy: The Interpretive Hermeneutic of Viktor Frankl

Ultimately, man should not ask what the meaning of his life is, but rather must recognize that it is he who is asked. And he can only answer to life by answering for his own life. Thus, logotherapy sees in responsibleness the very essence of human existence.
                                                   –Victor Frankl

Introduction
In recent years, Viktor E. Frankl, the Viennese psychiatrist who is the founder of what has come to be known as the Third Viennese School of Psychology – Freud and Adler constituting the founders of the other two schools – has emerged as the leading proponent in psychotherapeutic circles of the centrality of the experience of "meaning" in mental health. The goal of human life, Frankl has suggested, is to find meaning and order in the world for "me" personally and "us" collectively – both for me personally as an individual and for us all as a social consciousness seeking purpose and orderliness in our world. In this brief exploration, we will emulate David Bakan's now classic, *Sigmund Freud and the Jewish Mystical Tradition*, by identifying, within the framework of the Jewish mystical tradition, the sources and origins of Frank's scientific constructs in psychotherapy, and their manifestations in psycho-religious therapeutics.

The story is told of Schopenhauer who, customarily strolling through a Berlin park during the early hours of the morning in shabby clothes and sockless feet, was halted and questioned by a conscientious police officer: "Who are you? Where are you going?" To this our German philosopher answered true to form, "I wish to God I knew!" As this little story graphically illustrates, in modern times, life has become a struggle for reason and purpose. The sense of alienation which results in a concomitant sense of loss in personal identity and a growing recognition of an all-pervading estrangement from self and others, from personhood and neighborhood, from ego-identity and social identity, is so common that the feeling has become a cultural given. "The concept of meaning in all of its varieties," explains Suzanne Langer, "is the dominant philosophical concept of our time."[1]

Modern-day fixation upon, and bafflement over, our individual meaning – "the meaning of meaning" – is evidenced in every serious effort at the construction of a workable politic and social ethic. And yet, explains Heidegger, "no age has known so much, and so many different things, about man as ours... And no age has known less than ours of what man is."[2] In fact, in view of the current agitation over the need for an effective definition of humankind, we can honestly say we are in a "crisis of meaning." "We are the first epoch," corroborates Max Scheler, "in which man has become fully and thoroughly 'problematic' to himself; in which he no longer knows what he essentially is, but at the same time also knows that he does not know."[3]

In recent years, Viktor E. Frankl,[4] has emerged as the leading proponent in psychotherapeutic circles of the centrality of the experience of "meaning" in mental health.[5] Frankl dismissed Freud's inordinate emphasis upon the pleasure principle– what we might call here for the sake of symmetry the "will-to-pleasure" – contending that pleasure for the human person only has significance and purpose within the context of the individual's own grasp of life's meaning for oneself, i.e., life as personal. Furthermore, Frankl dismisses the Second Viennese School of Psychology, i.e., Alfred Adler and his notion of humankind's "will-to-power," by arguing that personal power in the face of suffering and in the absence of personal meaning has no visible function within the personality.[6]

The goal of human life, suggests Frankl, is to find meaning and order in the world for me personally and us collectively – both an individual and a social sense of purpose and orderliness in the world. Resulting from his heart-rending wartime Nazi concentration camp experience – where death and dying, suffering and inhumanity reigned supreme – Frankl became convinced of the *sui generus* nature of the *will-to-meaning*, what he later developed as logotherapy.[7] Amidst suffering and inhumanity, alienation and tragedy, he encountered the ever-impending onslaught of meaninglessness. Within the walls of an earthly human-made hell, an inhumanity which had taken his mother and wife and which threatened his own existence, he faced a stark nakedness of both body and soul the real possibility of the absence of any meaning to life. And yet, though the temptation for inmates to throw themselves upon the high voltage wires encircling the camp was ever present and often intense – indeed, even claiming the lives of some – nevertheless, most did not succumb to what Dostoyevski has diabolically referred to as the ultimate expression of human freedom, namely, suicide. In spite of unbelievable suffering and persecution, most camp inmates sought out and held on tenaciously to a sense of personal meaning in a world reduced to stark nothingness.

Sitting in the filth and hideousness of humanly contrived persecutions, where pain was omnipresent and death commonplace, Frankl's thoughts rose above his situation as he reflected upon the plight of others and himself. Later in life he wrote:

I remember my dilemma in the concentration camp

154

when faced with a man and a woman who were close to suicide; both had told me they expected nothing more of life. I asked both my fellow prisoners whether the question was really what we expected from life. Was it not, rather, what life was expecting from us? I suggested that life was awaiting something from them.[8]

As a result of Frankl's concentration camp experience at Auschwitz,[9] he discovered that our greatest need as personal beings is not the will-to-pleasure nor the will-to-power, but rather the will-to-meaning, the need to find meaning for one's own life. Through this discovery, and his utilization of this need in therapeutic situations, he developed what today is acclaimed as a major school in psychotherapy. By helping prisoners then, and patients later, remember their past lives – their joys, sorrows, sacrifices, and blessings – he emphasized the "meaningful-ness" of their lives as already lived.[10] During moments of apparent helplessness and meaninglessness, these recollections serve therapeutically to stabilize and reinforce the meaningfulness and purposefulness of life. He emphasizes not only the recollected past, but calls attention to the existential meaningfulness of suffering and tragedy in life as testimonies to human courage and dignity.[11]

In logotherapy, Frankl differentiates meaning and values.[12] Values are socially held meanings whereas meaning as the *sine qua non* of life is a unique experience and possession of every single individual in every moment of one's own life. Frankl contended that this will-to-meaning – as Freud argued for "pleasure" and Adler for "power" – pervades every theatrical stage as well as every secret recess of one's personal life. Meaning, he pointed out, can be found in any situation within which we finds ourselves.[13] The concentration camp inmates could live only if they could make sense – will-to-meaning – out of their apparently senseless suffering. The fact that they lived and survived to tell of it speaks empirically enough of this will-to-meaning. Where human life exists, there meaning is to be found.

The surprising feature about Frankl's psychotherapeutic formulations is that throughout he consistently makes inferential comments about the religious dynamic operative in his theory while constantly omitting any specific reference to its fundamentally Jewish character.[14] Especially does he consistently fail to refer, even at most commodious opportunities, to the presence of a strong element of Hassidic teachings, i.e., the teachings of the rabbis who rose up in the eighteenth century in Eastern Europe in reaction against an overemphasis on talmudic learning and radical mystical Messianism.

If David Bakan is even tacitly correct in his attribution of a religious infrastructure to Sigmund Freud's psychological formulations, we cannot be far wrong in the identification of major Jewish principles in Victor Frankl's psychology.[15] As Freud utilized, whether consciously or not, the conceptual frameworks of the Hassidic book of mysticism, the *ZOHAR*, so Frankl unquestionably used the philosophical teachings of the Hassidic rabbis in his consideration of life's meaning.[16] And yet, nowhere does Frankl face frankly the legitimate philosophical question: "From whence comes this meaning?" Is it a human contrivance *a la* Sartre, or is it a discovery *a la* Kierkegaard? Frankl answers with the latter, but gives no satisfactory explanation as to the origin or source of this meaning. However, appropriate to this discussion, Fackenheim supplies us with a genuinely religious view of the Jewish perception of this quandary. "In the eyes of

Judaism, whatever meaning life acquires derives from this encounter: The Divine accepts and confirms the human in the moment of meeting. But the meaning conferred upon human life by the Divine-human encounter cannot be understood in terms of some finite purpose, supposedly more ultimate than the meeting itself. For what could be more ultimate than the Presence of God?"[17] For the religiously sensitive Jewish thinker, humankind cannot simply be satisfied with the discovery of meaning for oneself, but must plumb deeper for the source of all meaning. The Presence of God, Buber has explained, is an "*inexpressible* confirmation of meaning... The question of the meaning of life is no longer there (when God is Present). But were it there, it would not have to be answered."[18] And though we would not wish to fault Frankl prematurely or unfairly, we might have rightfully expected from a Viennese Jewish psychiatrist an expression of his sensibility to the philosophical problem implied in his psychology and the source of his philosophical perspective in addressing these problems.

The therapeutic efficacy of his logotherapy is not open to question, but accountability for its rational basis must be pondered. As we have considered at length in another place, we are not simply satisfied with an ontological answer to our existential query, "Who am I?," for we are also in pursuit of the source of the answer when it does come, whether it is contrived or discovered. That Frankl is indebted to Jewish teaching is without question. "What Frankl calls 'logotherapy' and the 'will to meaning,'" explains Rubenstein, himself a rather critical Jewish philosopher of the post-Auschwitzian variety, "is not unlike the striving for an ordered, meaningful cosmos on the part of the rabbinic teachers in their own times."[19] Rubenstein believes that for Frankl, this reaching back into his own religious heritage, i.e., the Hassidic tradition of Viennese

Judaism, constituted the only basis upon which Frankl could ever hope to decipher the ultimate meaning of the concentration camp horrors. Without such a legacy, Frankl and his fellow inmates would have surely succumbed. "Only by resorting to the age-old Jewish interpretation of misfortune," explains Rubenstein, "could he (Frankl) maintain his sanity." That Rubenstein is correct in his conclusion is certainly open to discussion (and in my personal opinion he is doing little more than attempting to disparage Frankl's religious faith in the wake of his own faithlessness), but that Frankl's psychology and Jewish philosophy are intertwined is indisputable.

In Frankl's logotherapy, not only is the human person portrayed as being in possession of a *sense of meaningfulness* but also of a personal *sense of indebtedness*.[20] Not only is life charged with meaning, this meaning implies responsibility. Life is for me meaningful and I, therefore, must respond. Life provides an arena within which I must discover meaning, and this discovery places *upon me* "an expectation *of me*." Let us quote Frankl exactly on this point:

Ultimately, man should not ask what the meaning of his life is, but rather must recognize that it is *he* who is asked. In a word, each man is questioned by life; and he can only answer to life by *answering for* his own life; to life he can only respond by being responsible. Thus, logotherapy sees in responsibleness the very essence of human existence.

To demonstrate the fundamentally religious character of Frankl's psychology, we need only look to the writings of Rabbi Abraham Joshua Heschel who is without question America's most respected Jewish philosopher in the past century. "The dimension of meaning," says Heschel, "is as indigenous to his (mankind's) being human as the dimension of space is to stars and stones...Human being is either coming into meaning or betraying it."[21] In other words, all of human life is a struggle to maintain a relationship to meaning, and though this relationship ebbs and flows with the rise and fall of our conscientious quest for meaning or our recalcitrant niggardliness in seeking it, humankind is continually confronted with the choice of meaning or meaninglessness. Heschel explains further:

Imbedded in the mind is a certainty that the state of existence and the sate of meaning stand in relation to each other, that life is accessible in terms of meaning. The *will to meaning* and the certainty of the legitimacy of our striving to ascertain it are as intrinsically human as the will to live and the certainty of being alive.

Heschel offers a clarification to the ambiguity suggested in Frankl's perception of meaning – from where does it derive and who is it for? If meaning is derived from within ourselves and is strictly for our personal aggrandizement, we are no better off than Freud's pleasure seeker, Adler's power seeker, or Sartre's pathetic drunkard who chose freely not to serve his fellow man. "What we are in search of," clarifies Heschel, "is not meaning for me, an idea to satisfy my conscience, but rather a meaning transcending me, ultimate relevance for being human."

Let us consider more carefully this dual sense of meaning and indebtedness, alluded to in Frankl and explicated in Heschel. What Frankl faced in the camps and what we all confront at various moments in our lives is the immanence of despair, of forlornness, of a sense of nothingness. "There is not a soul on this earth," contends Heschel, "which has not realized that life is dismal if not mirrored in something which is lasting."[22] Heschel's criticism of Sartre and Nietzsche is precisely here – we are not our own measure. "Tell man he is an end within himself," warns Heschel, "and his answer will be despair." As human beings, we are not our own judge and jury and "despair is not (our) last word," says Heschel, nor is "hiddenness God's last act."[23]

Though Heschel agrees that humankind is fundamentally "a being in search of meaning," unlike Frankl, he is not satisfied in stopping at that observation. To the biblical mind, explains Heschel, "man is not only a creature who is constantly in search of himself, but also *a creature God is constantly in search of.*" Furthermore, says Heschel, "man is a creature in search of meaning because there is meaning in search of him, because there is God's beseeching question, 'Where art thou?'" Here is the juncture at which Frankl's psychology must give way to Jewish philosophy – where meaning no longer is an *a priori* given but an explanation of a prior relationship which exists between God and humankind. The meaning of human life derives from the source of all meaning – "God is in need of man... To Jewish religion, history is determined by this covenant."[24] Religion, culminating in its Jewish expression, consists of God's question --"Where art though?," and in the human answer – "I was afraid" (Gen. 3: 9-10). Personal meaning derives from God, and God, in turn, is searching for the human person.

It is with this insight, suggests Heschel, that we can come to a better understanding of our own nature. Meaning does not derive from humankind for humankind does not produce meaning, neither can we look to ourselves in hopes of understanding the nature of meaning. "Man is man," explains Heschel, "not because of what he has in common with the earth, but *because of what he has in common with God.*"[25] Humankind cannot endow the sky with stars, neither can we bestow upon ourselves inalienable rights. Equality of humankind is not due to humankind's own ingenuity, but rather "is due to *God's love and commitment to all men*...(For) wherever you see a trace of man, there is the presence of God."

Only when we lift our sights above frivolities, inhumanity and selfishness, can we hope to sense the meaning of life, for, says Heschel, "the destiny of man is to be a partner of God."[26] This, says he, is the "main event in Israel's history," namely, "God's search for man." It is here we see the underpinnings of Frankl's psychology of the will-to-meaning. The person seeks meaning because meaning seeks the person. "This," says Heschel, "is the central message of the biblical prophets. God is involved in the life of man." And with this, we can move from our extrapolation of the "sense of meaning" expressed in Frankl to his emphasis upon a concomitant "sense of indebtedness" resulting from this discovery of meaning. Frankl's appeal to a sense of meaning, while caring for his fellow inmates, rested upon his capacity to elicit from them a sense of life's expectations of them. Legitimate human existence consists not in my expectations of life but of life's rightful expectations of me.

But from where do these "rightful expectations" come? Surely not from within ourselves, suggests Frankl, for just as certainly as we cannot generate our own meaning, neither can one hope to generate one's own expectations. Furthermore, under such circumstances, how could any ethic exist? When we become our own source of expectations, our animality, not our humanity, comes to the fore, Heschel contends. We need only witness again the rise of Nazi Germany! To unravel this quandary, from "whence comes" human meaning, Heschel explains that "man is man because something is at stake in his existence." This sense of a requiredness of human existence is fundamental to all of humankind, and in religious life, humankind moves beyond isolation from self and into communion with God.

"Religion," explains Heschel, "begins with a

consciousness that something is asked of us." With this, we must read Frankl's therapeutic efforts at making individuals aware of life's expectations of them as essentially religious and pastoral in nature. Not that we would belittle this function. Quite the contrary, to the extent that Frankl's logotherapy functions to put individuals in touch with life's meaning and its implied debt, we can rightfully expect from him an allegiance to his own religious heritage. "The essence of Judaism," says Heschel, "is the awareness of the reciprocity of God and man, of man's *togetherness* with Him...(for) Man does not exist apart from God. The human is the borderline of the divine."

In Judaism, explains Heschel, "man cannot think of himself as human without being conscious of his indebtedness."[27] For Heschel, as for Shopenhauer's police officer, human consciousness rises to religious sensibilities at the point of asking "Who am I?" and "What am I to do?" "Religious consciousness," says Heschel, "is to be characterized by two features – it must be a consciousness of *an ultimate commitment* and it must be a consciousness of *ultimate reciprocity*." The "is-ness" of human meaning is complimented by the "oughtness" of religious consciousness. And the ultimate expression of this consciousness in the "Jewish religion...is the *awareness of God's interest in man*, the awareness of a *covenant*, of a reciprocity that lies on Him as well as on us."

In this discussion, we have seen how Frankl's logotherapy, which is a psychotherapeutic method employed to assist individuals in getting in touch with life's meaning and its implied indebtedness, relies heavily upon the Hassidic tradition within Jewish philosophy most recently extrapolated in the writings of Abraham Joshua Heschel. We have not attempted to indict Frankl as a rabbinic teacher in psychiatric garb, but rather have attempted to vindicate Frankl's logotherapy from the appearance of being devoid of philosophical underpinnings. Further, we have attempted to indicate that his psychology is quite defensible both in terms of existential psychology and Jewish philosophy. Frankl's theory, it seems, is thus rendered stronger, thanks to its identifiable philosophical defensibility witnessed in Heschel's grasp and use of the Hassidic tradition. To draw from one's own faith tradition for insight into the mysterious workings of the human mind cannot be a bad thing, and to patiently wait for the effectiveness of the insight might well serve those in pastoral counseling. As my on teacher, Rabbi Samuel Sandmel, was often heard to say: "Grace delayed is not grace denied." Rabbinic wisdom and scientific insight may very well have found a profound convergence in the logotherapeutic construct of Viktor Frankl.

ENDNOTES

1 Suzanne K. Langer, *Philosophical Sketches* (New York: Mentor, 1964), p. 54.

2 Martin Heidegger, *Kant and The Problems of Metaphysics* (Bloomington, IN: Indiana University Press, 1962), p. xxi.

3 As quoted in Martin Buber, *Between Man and Man* (New York: Macmillan, 1968), p. 182.

4 Frankl's major works include, *From Death Camp To Existentialism* (Boston: Press, 1959); *The Doctor and The Soul: An Introduction To Logotherapy* (New York: Alfred A. Knopf, 1963), and *Man's Search For Meaning* (New York: Washington Square Press, 1964).

5 See Viktor E. Frankl, "Psychiatry and Man's Quest for Meaning," *Journal of Religion and Health*, Vol. 1, pp.

93-103, 1962.

6 Viktor E. Frankl, "Logotherapy and the Challenge of Suffering," *Pastoral Psychology*, Vol. 13, pp. 25-28, 1962.

7 Viktor E. Frankl, "The Will to Meaning," *The Journal of Pastoral Care*, Vol. 12, pp. 82- 88, 1958.

8 Frankl, *Man's Search For Meaning*, pp. 12-13.

9 See Frankl, Pt. One, "Experience in a Concentration Camp," in *Man's Search For Meaning*, pp. 3f.

10 Viktor E. Frankl, "Group Psychotherapeutic Experiences in a Concentration Camp," *Group Psychotherapy*, Vol. 7, pp. 81-90, 1954.

11 Viktor E. Frankl, "Logotherapy and the Challenge of Suffering," *Review of Existential Psychology and Psychiatry*, Vol. 1, pp. 3-7, 1961.

12 Viktor E. Frankl, "Dynamics, Existence and Values," *Journal of Existential Psychiatry*, Vol. 2, pp. 5-16, 1961.

13 Viktor E. Frankl, "Logos and Existence in Psychotherapy," *American Journal of Psychotherapy*, Vol. 7, pp. 8-15, 1953.

14 Cf. Viktor E. Frankl, "The Spiritual Dimension in Existential Analysis and Logotherapy," *Journal of Individual Psychology*, Vol. 15, pp. 157-165, 1957, and Viktor E. Frankl, "Religion and Existential Psychotherapy," *The Gordon Review*, Vol. 6, pp. 2- 10, 1961.

15   Frankl, *Man's Search For Meaning*, pp. 154, 156, 157.

16   Frankl has paid at least passing attention to the philosophical implications of his work,   but   not specifically to Hassidism. Cf. Victor E. Frankl. "Psychotherapy and   Philosophy," *Philosophy Today*, Vol. 5, pp. 59-64, 1961. Chapter Two.

17   Emil L. Fackenheim. *Quest For Past and Future: Essays In Jewish Theology.* (Boston: Beacon Press, 1970), p. 245.

18   Martin Buber, *I and Thou* (New York: Charles Scribner's, 1958), p. 110.

19   Richard L. Rubenstein, *The   Religious Imagination: A Study In Psychoanalysis And   Jewish Philosophy* (Boston: Beacon, 1968), p. 177.

20   Frankl, *Man's Search For Meaning*, p. 13: "...The question was really what...life was   expecting from us."

21   Abraham J. Heschel, *Who Is Man?* (Stanford: University Press, 1968), p. 50.

22   Abraham J. Heschel, *Man Is Not Alone: A Philosophy Of Religion* (New York: Farrar,   Straus,   and Giroux, 1972), p. 198.

23   Abraham J. Heschel, *Israel: An Echo Of Eternity* (New York: Farrar, Straus, and Giroux,   1974), p. 135.

24   Heschel, *Between God And Man*, p. 51.

25   Heschel, *The Insecurity of Freedom*, p. 152.

26   Abraham J. Heschel, *God In Search Of Man: A Philosophy Of Judaism* (New York: Harper Torchbooks, 1966), p. 312.

27   Abraham J. Heschel, *A Passion For Truth* (New York: Farrar, Straus, and Giroux, 1974),   p. 259.

CHAPTER TEN
Cognitive Behavioral Therapy and Reminiscence Therapy in the Treatment of Depression:
A Convergent Palliative Care Methodology in Geriatric Psychotherapy

Geriatric psychotherapy within the health care professions (Arean, Hegel, Vannoy, Fan, and Unutzer, 2008; Ayeers, Sorrell, Thorp, and Wetherell, 2007; Landreville, Laudry, Baillargeon, Guerette, and Mattewa, 2001) including, and of particular interest to us here, palliative psychotherapeutic care has in recent years become an increasingly important component of comprehensive health care treatment options. There are a large number of counselors and psychotherapists as well as psychiatrists, however, who find themselves with an increase in post-retirement clients and patients but without the benefit of specific training in treating this particular constituency (Karel, Ogland-Hand, Gatz, and Unuetzer, 2002; Gatz, Fiske, Fox, Kaskie, Kasl-Godley, and McCallum, 1999; Hinrichsen, 2008). There is a large population of older individuals in need of assistance in dealing with depression and its cognates of anxiety and self-esteem issues which are of particular concern to the health care profession working in palliative care medicine (Stanley, Wilson, Novy, Rhoades, Wagener, Greisinger, 2009; Knight and McCallum, 1998).

Neither psychotherapeutic nor biological psychiatry has made a name for itself in developing new approaches to the treatment of depression among the palliative care patient community. However, what is now being called palliative care psychiatry is on the rise as an emerging subspecialty where palliative medicine and psychiatry converge (Fairman and Irwin, 2013). The interfacing of palliative care medicine with psychiatry is being heralded throughout the medical community as a positive step forward in the development of modalities of treatment, both pharmacologically-linked and psychotherapeutic, which may be further researched and evidence-based tested for efficacy.

That there is a relative void in the training of palliative care health professionals in geriatric psychotherapy, particularly as relates to the treatment of depression, is very evident according to recent AMA-sponsored studies (Gallagher-Thompson and Steffen, 1994). In the following essay, we will consider briefly two evidence-based treatment options available to the counseling and psychotherapeutic community dealing particularly with palliative psychotherapeutic depression, namely, Cognitive Behavioral Therapy (CBT) and Reminiscence Therapy (RT) (Scogin and McElreath, 1994). Following this brief discussion, we will explore the integration of CBT and RT into a single treatment modality used in palliative care of the elderly suffering from debilitating depression. Five brief case studies will be presented as illustrations of its use and effectiveness as reported in recent clinical studies. As we know, biogenic depression calls for pharmacological intervention and, therefore, medical oversight. However, our interest here is rather to call attention to two proven modalities of treatment available for the non-medically trained psychotherapist dealing with palliative psychogenic depression (Knight and Qualls, 2006). There are several modalities of treatment for late-life depression for both institutionalized patients and those living at home (Francis and Kumar, 2013) including cognitive and behavioral therapy, problem-solving therapy, reminiscence and life review therapy, brief psychodynamic therapy, and interpersonal therapy. These studies are consistently showing evidence-based findings validating the use of each of these modalities of treatment of depression and depressive symptoms in older adults.

There are consistent evidence-based studies showing that non-pharmacological interventions offer the prospects of reducing cognitive decline in late life depression patients as well as the improvement of psychosocial aspects of older individuals suffering from mild cognitive impairment along with well as Alzheimer's dementia (Herholz, Herholz, and Herholz, 2013). The absence of side effects owing to the non-pharmacological therapies employed make those therapies attractive options for the therapist, the patient, and the family involved. Recent studies will be reviewed here including those involving cognitive training and reminiscence including such components as visual arts and music, physical activities, and electromagnetic stimulation.

Specific treatment modalities which have an evidence-based effectiveness record to date include Cognitive Behavior Therapy (Barrowclough, King, Colville, Russell, Burns, and Tarrier, 2001; Cappeliez, 2001; Siskin, 2002), Brief Dynamic Therapy (Messer, 2001), Interpersonal Psychotherapy (Hinrichsen and Clougherty, 2006), Reminiscence Therapy (Bohlmeijer, Smit, and Cuijpers, 2003), and Geriatric Logotherapy (Morgan, 2012a). These are commonly used by non-medically oriented psychotherapists and professional counselors in palliative health care facilities and, as will be indicated, have proven consistently to be effective tools for therapy in dealing with older clients as illustrated by evidence-based empirical studies (Arean and Ayalon, 2005). Our interest here, however, is in CBT asnd RT and the convergence of these two methods of treating depression among elderly palliative care patents.

Behavioral therapies, particularly Cognitive Behavioral Therapy (CBT) and Rational Emotive Behavior Therapy (REBT), being the most used modalities of treating non-medical or psychogenic depression among older clients have the largest data-base evidence for effectiveness (Floyd and Scogin, 1998). Depression is considered within the cognitive behavioral school of psychotherapy to essentially constitute the inability of the individual to cope with stress brought on by the aging process itself including such things as problem solving skills, isolation within the social matrix of daily living, and the decline in physical skills capabilities (King, Heisel, and Lyness, 2005). The emphasis in these CBT treatment options focuses upon the practicalities of skill enhancement and the intentionality in the reorientation towards life stressors by reconfiguring the client's daily schedule, priorities, and inclinations (Gatz, 2007). CBT and its variants have proven very effective in facilitating the older client, post-retirement particularly, in redefining one's life situation, the *Sitz im Lebcn*, to accommodate a new understanding of one's relationship to the social environment of interpersonal relationships, life skills, and self-satisfaction. Evidence is strong for the overwhelming success of CBT compared to other modalities of depression treatment versus wait-list controls and no treatment at all (Floyd and Scogin, 1998; Siskin, 2002). And, this evidential data demonstrates that CBT has a longevity value beyond that of pharmacological treatments as well (Hyer, Hilton, Sacks, Freidman, and Yeager, 2009). The CBT agenda is two-fold, viz., to reduce the psychogenic depression and to elevate the social interaction and the physical skills-based functioning of the client. Reduction of depressive behavior while increasing social and physical activity constitutes the treatment agenda of CBT, and the evidence for its effectiveness is substantial (Stanley, Wilson, Novy, Rhoades, Wagener, Greisinger, and et al., 2009).

Cognitive Behavioral Therapy (CBT) is based essentially upon the cognitive model proposing that thoughts, feelings, and behaviors are interconnected and that any improvement in the emotional life of a troubled individual can only occur when the client is able to overcome his difficulties by acknowledging, identifying, and addressing dysfunctional ideas and thoughts as well as counter-productive behaviors and distressing emotional responses to life's situations (Cappeliez, 2001). CBT suggests that thoughts, feelings, and behavior constitute a tripartite inter-dependence, each affecting the other in both positive and negative ways (Landreville, Laudry, Baillargeon, Guerette, and Matteau, 2001). Re-directing cognition, or how an individual thinks about himself, the world, and the future, constitutes the primary mechanism by means of which long-term emotional and behavioral desirable and self-affirming changes can take place. The relationship between the therapist and the client is one of aggressive interaction involving a collaborative reliance upon the development of a re-configuration and re-conceptualization of the client's worldview and strategized behavioral response to it (Barrowclough, King, Colville, Russell, Burns, and Tarrier, 2001).

Cognitive Behavioral Therapy (CBT) is a long established approach to the treatment of dysfunctional emotions, maladaptive behaviors and cognitive processes and contents through the use of a variety of goal-oriented, explicit systematic procedures. The focus is upon therapies dealing with cognitive and behavioral issues in which the patient is led to understand that the dysfunctional emotions and resulting behavior, such as debilitating depression among the elderly, has to do with the cognitive aspects of perception and recollection of the interpersonal encounters from which distorted reactions derive (Landreville, Laudry, Baillargeon, Guerette, and Matteau, 2001; Macklin and Arean, 2005). By "blending" or "collapsing" the patient's remembered experience with a redefined or reconstructed understanding of these distorted experiences, the patient is led to a more positive and self-affirming explication of those experiences. Problem-solving approaches employed by CBT focus upon thought-processes or strategies for the patient in reconfiguring otherwise negative and disempowering remembrances and recollections towards more nurturing and promising understanding. CBT has consistently demonstrated its effectiveness in treating such emotionally charged conditions as mood swings, anxiety, personality dysfunctions, eating disorders, substance abuse, and most effective of all in the treatment of debilitating depression. Evidence-based verification of effectiveness is common, and CBT has become the most favored approach to symptom-based diagnoses in psychodynamic treatment plans (Chambless and Hollon, 1998; Gatz, Fiske, Fox, Kaskie, Kasl-Godley, and McCallum, 1999; Bartels, Dums, Oxman, et al., 2002).

In addition to Cognitive Behavioral Therapy, we are suggesting that it be blended with Reminiscence Therapy (RT) for a creative composition of both cognitive behavior and memory. RT is recognized by the American Psychological Association as "the use of life histories – written, oral, or both – to improve psychological well-being. The therapy is often used with older people." Consistently effective by evidence-based studies in palliative care of the elderly, RT has been most beneficial in the treatment of debilitating depression among the elderly particularly in palliative care settings. What is called the Webster

Reminiscence Functions Scale (RFS) looks particularly at eight specific reasons why older people have a tendency to reminisce, and the purpose of RT is to address these reasons with therapeutic intent. They include boredom reduction, bitterness revival, preparation for death, conversation, identity, intimacy maintenance, problem solving, and teaching/informing others (Morgan, 2011; Morgan, 2012d; Morgan, 2012e). RT has been consistently beneficial in psychotherapeutic usage, and what we are suggesting here is combined with CBT's emphasis upon reconfiguring cognitive behavioral dysfunctions such as distorted recollections. The emotional benefit for the palliative care elderly patient has proven significant (Morgan, 2013a).

Studies (Connell, 1988) are now regularly providing evidence-based data to validate the effectiveness of Reminiscence Therapy (RT) used in the treatment of geriatric depression within the nursing home institutional setting. RT is a non-pharmacological intervention involving the prompting of past memories on the part of the palliative care patient. Clearly the most prevalent mental health disorder among institutionalized elderly is that of depression. What is important in the Connell study is the use of RT "intermittently" rather than as the one primary modality of treatment employed once. Data is now showing that periodic, spaced, intermittent uses of RT have a greater evidence-based benefit.

Systematic assessment of the use of Reminiscence Therapy (RT) in the treatment of patients suffering from minor as well as major dementia (Dempsey, Murphy, Cooney, Casey, O'Shea, Devane, Jordan, and Hunter, 2014) reveals that there is currently no consistent definition of RT within the healthcare literature or professional practice. There is, however, a consistency of characteristics of the various definitional parameters of the term and its usage.

There is a systemic divergence in the goals, theory base, and content of the competing definitional matrices of RT practice including the use of such terms as life review, early life events, remembered childhood relationships, etc. However, universally agreed upon components of RT include stages of life, age, life transitional events, attention span issues, recall ability over time, vocalizations including tunes, and remembered stress situations. These studies demonstrate the common usage of RT in the treatment of dementia showing effective results in enhancement of self-esteem, improved communication skills, self-worthy personal identity and a sense of individuality.

To date, studies of meta-analysis focusing on psychosocial interventions have failed to address specific treatment of individual Behavioral and Psychological Symptoms of Dementia (BPSD) involving personalized interventions. Based on 641 care home and nursing home studies involving cluster randomized controlled trials as well as pre- and post-test studies (Testad, Corbett, Aarsland, Lexow, Fossey, Woods, and Ballard, 2014), good evidence supporting the use of Reminiscence Therapy in improving mood swings and a diminishment of agitation is being regularly and systematically found.

The benefits of Reminiscence Therapy (RT) for the improvement of the quality of life of individuals, both in and out of institutionalized care facilities, suffering from dementia has consistently produced evidence-based validation. However, the value of RT for care givers has yet to be researched and documented (Melunsky, Crellin, Dudzinski, Orrell, Wenborn, Poland, Woods, and Charlesworth, 2014). Based on a recent study of 18 family care givers involved in group sessions, the evidence for effectiveness in enhancing their skills in interacting with dementia patients proved inconclusive with the suggestion that further study is needed. Without further study and evidence-based findings, the suggestion is that there is little justification in the continuation of joint reminiscence groups in dementia care (Knight and McCallum, 1998; Knight, 1999).

Owing to the acute adaptation difficulties of older individuals being institutionalized for palliative care, the emergence of depression and cognates including agitation, apathy, and the onset of minor dementia symptoms as well as a diminishment of a feeling of general well-being is proving consistently evident in nursing home reports (Melendez-Moral, Charco-Ruiz, Mayordomo-Rodriguez, and Sales-Galan, 2013). Reminiscence Therapy (RT) has consistently proven to be among the most effective non-pharmacological intervention modalities of palliative care treatment with a minimum of debilitating side-effects while maximizing the reduction of these depressive symptoms.

In spite of the frequency of reports of effectiveness in the use of Reminiscence Therapy (RT) in the treatment of depression and dementia among the institutionalized elderly population (Klever, 2013), there is a conspicuous absence of actual research evidence addressing the specifics of the connection between reminiscence functions and the reduction of depressive symptoms (Hallford, Mellor, and Cummins, 2013). The Hallford and colleagues' study tests the hypothesis regarding the "indirect associations of adaptive integrative and instrumental reminiscence functions with depressive symptoms," addressing the question regarding whether or not these relationship might differ from younger to older patients. This study of 730 younger and 725 older individuals provided evidence-based validation of the effectiveness of RT in the treatment of both age groups in the reduction of depression and depressive symptoms including having substantive impacts upon meaning of life issues, self-esteem, and personal optimism about the future.

With both the rise of dementia and psychogenic depression among the over-65 year old population in the U.S. which continues to rise exponentially owing to the baby-boomers, there is evidence of an increasing need for more responsive evidence-based validated psychotherapeutic modalities of treatment (Morgan, 2015). Reminiscence Therapy (RT) is proving to be one of those which is providing evidence-based validation of its effectiveness. As clinicians are discovering, when this modality of treatment is supplemented with the use of "technologies" as explored by Lazar and team (Lazar, Thompson, and Demiris, 2014), such things as photographic artifacts as well as period-based music used in the facilitation of social interaction within groups as well as individual treatment plans is gaining support within the counseling and psychotherapeutic communities, the positive results are most impressive. A diminishment of depression and a documented rise in self-esteem are two prevalent benefits of the use of these material supplements called Information and Communication Technologies (ICT). Another benefit documented in these evidence-based studies is that of patients actually taking ownership of conversations in both group settings and with one-on-one relationships with a family member, therapist, or care giver (Pasacreta and Pickett, 1998). The use of what are referred to as multimedia reminiscence materials also results, according to these studies, in the reduction of barriers to motor deficits in the behavioral interaction.

A specific study of male veterans (Chue and Chang, 2014) utilizing Group Reminiscence Therapy (GRT) was conducted in a nursing facility's intervention program evaluating 3-month and 6-month effects on depressive symptoms for institutionalized veterans. Following a 4-week intervention, the evidence-based findings validated the effectiveness of this treatment plan based on reduced depressive symptoms. This increasingly popular variation on Reminiscence Therapy, i.e., Group Reminiscence Therapy (GRT), is commonly used within a group of age peers suffering from psychogenic depression in an institutional setting such as a residential nursing home. GRT functions as a brief and structured intervention treatment modality and according to Gaggioli and colleagues (Gaggioli, Scaratti, Morganti, Stramba-Badiale, Agostoni, Spatola, Molinari, Cipresso, and Riva, 2014), it is proving with evidence-based demonstrations increased effectiveness for group therapy beyond its already validated effectiveness with individuals.

The blending of treatment modalities in the care of the elderly suffering from depression is most common and what is being suggested and illustrated here is simply one instance of a combining of two treatment modalities, CBT and RT, with a heavy emphasis upon the palliative care of the elderly patient suffering from debilitating depression (Satre, Knight, and David, 2006). As neither CBT nor RT are pharmacologically based treatments, we will address ourselves strictly to the psychogenic depressive symptoms of the elderly in palliative care with an emphasis upon the existential nature of care, namely, the goal is not cure but nurture of the terminally ill older patient. Both cognitive behavior and the act of reminiscing constitute a paralleling of reflective self-consciousness, the former addressing an understanding of the behavioral what and why and the latter addressing the recollection and memory of life events. To combine both the behavioral matrix of self-awareness with reflections upon past events seems a natural coupling of two conscious processes operative within the human mind and susceptible to therapeutic intervention. Since CBT strives to assist the patient in understanding an event or occurrence in his/her life which has produced a depressive reaction, the aim is to revisit that event with the aim of reconfiguring it or reconstructing it with a more positive understanding and outcome. Reminiscence Therapy, likewise, encourages the patient to reflect upon past events and occurrences with the aim of identifying those which offer nurture and positive memory responses and to de-sensitize those events which conjure upon negative feelings and emotions. In both instances, CBT and RT, the aim is to so reconstruct the remembered past such that it serves as a *repertoire* or *reservoir* of nurturing memories.

Illustrative of the use and effectiveness of this combination of CBT and RT approaches the case of Mrs. Williams, a nursing home patient in her mid-80s suffering from acute and near debilitating depression. Other complicating health issues include high blood pressure, diabetes, and arthritis. A retired librarian for some twenty-plus years, Mrs. Williams came to the nursing home after falling in her home where she lived alone. The decision was made for institutional care in conjunction with family members (all distant cousins as she was widowed with no children). In meeting with her over several sessions, the therapist struggled with finding the "door of happy memories" through which to follow Mrs. Williams. Finally, during the third clinical session, some passing reference was made to her childhood farm life and swimming with her girlfriends in the cow pond behind the barn. As this passing reference seemed to cause her to pause and smile as she was formulaically reciting her life's story to the therapist, it became clear to the observing therapist that she enjoyed the memory and might enjoy elaborating upon it. The result was a meandering recollection of her childhood experiences with her friends on the family farm which, she said, "I haven't thought of in years." Subsequent sessions always harped back to these happy memories and provided a substance to her solitary reflections beyond the therapy sessions.

Often, the geriatric patient needs assistance in conjuring these past episodes of happiness and the therapist then can employ what I have chosen to call "memory suggestions," viz., asking the individual to backtrack consciously in search of illustrative events in his or her life to which they themselves attribute a blissful and happy experience. However, an important key here for the therapist to keep in mind is "stress avoidance," that is, redirecting the individual away from remembered events in their past which clearly, by facial expression or voice intonation, suggest stress or anxiety or unhappiness (Morgan, 2010). Family history is quite frequently the source of these happiness episodes, but the therapist is advised to watch carefully lest the family history stories drift downward into negative memories.

It is crucial that the therapist keep in mind the logotherapeutic agenda lest one imagine that the purpose and goal of the therapeutic session is to search out the "meaning and purpose of life" yet to be lived. With the older and elderly patient, the acutely practical nature of the existential utility and viability of therapy must always be kept in the forefront of the therapeutic encounter. Though sometimes a challenge in dealing with the elderly (geriatric dementia often manifests itself in the individual's disinclination to converse), the therapist must employ what I have chosen to call "points of conversation" as an impetus and incentive for the geriatric patient to engage the therapist in the quest for existential episodes of happiness (Morgan, 1987). Places, times, and people constitute for me the three fundamental arenas within which the patient may find these points of conversation leading to the "discovery" and "revisiting" of happiness episodes in their earlier life.

Another example of this geriatric psychotherapeutic approach is the case of Dr. Watson, a retired philosophy professor living alone in his home as a widower having two adult children living far away. Dr. Watson is in his late 80s, was once a nationally recognized scholar, author of several books, but these days finds reading increasingly difficult owing to glaucoma while writing is virtually impossible due to arthritis in both hands. Reduced to sitting on his expansive front porch when weather permits and before the fireplace otherwise, Dr. Watson has sunk into a debilitating depression resulting in a consistent failure to eat regularly or to converse over the phone with friends and family. A concerned son precipitated the contact with a therapist who made an initial home visit, finding the above situation. Dr. Watson had essentially "given up," as he put it, because of an inability to read or write which was his life's work and passion. When the therapist encouraged the professor to "tell me about your life's work," Dr. Watson commenced slowly and deliberately rattling off his educational background, teaching appointments, books written, conferences attended, all with little passion and near expressionless. However, when the therapist asked about specific colleagues mentioned in the monotone narrative, he noticed that the patient became somewhat animated, enthusiastic, even excited to relate story after story involving colleagues, happy stories, fun stories, all leading to an extremely productive journey through time and people of importance. Subsequent sessions centered upon the same topics with the result that Dr. Watson began calling old friends, inviting other retired colleagues in town to come for morning coffee and chat. The door of happy memories had been opened and entered and Dr. Watson's life took on renewed vitality.

One of the greatest challenges for the therapist is to acknowledge and own the inevitable reality of the brevity of life left to the elderly patient. The palliative therapeutic goal here is clearly not some form of contrived cure for what might be the presenting symptoms of depression which is most commonly the driving force in seeking help for the patient either by the patient or the family or residential institutional staff responsible for caring for the patient. A cure certainly is not what is sought here, but rather, beyond and after the notion of a cure for the aged patient, there is an urgent need for the identification of the rightful place for palliative care in such situations. A quest for existential happiness, episodic joys in happy memories, constitutes the driving force in the therapeutic encounter with the geriatric patient who most commonly is suffering from depression.

A concluding illustration of the value of geriatric psychotherapy and its use in existential counseling of the depressed patient is the case of Miss Horton, an elderly spinster school teacher from a small town, whose life had been synonymous with teaching elementary school children, living in the background, watching them grow up, move away, establish families, and launch careers. Now nearly 90 years old residing in an assisted living facility in her little town, she had drifted into depression owing to a lack of social stimulus (most other residents were suffering from acute and severely debilitating geriatric dementia). Her health had declined gradually owing to heart problems and towards the end of her life, she had taken to the bed and was less and less willing to converse with even the nurses. The nursing director called in the therapist (based on the therapist's reputation in dealing with geriatric dementia), and from the beginning the initial encounter was fruitless, boarding on hopeless. As the therapist explored Miss Horton's social life through interviews with nursing staff who knew the patient's personal history and in the therapist's search for the "magic door" that would introduce happy memories and reflective thoughts of joys gone by, it occurred to him that since her life had been lived for the children she taught, why not get some of those children, now adults, to come say goodbye to her in her closing days of life. It worked wonders. Through the local school, the therapist was able to contact several of her past students, now parents and successful people, to come for a visit. Since most people are uncomfortable visiting someone on their death bed, the therapist always arranged to be present, coaching the visitor to help Miss Horton remember episodes in the classroom and on the playground in which she was a major player and to share with her, as she lay mute but alert, the stories of their own lives as they left school and entered the world, always with reference to her contribution to their own personal lives. The results were remarkable, not that she lived much longer, for she did not, but during the closing weeks of her life, she became conversant, sitting up in bed, asking about this student and that student, remembering to the therapist more and more "happy moments" in her teaching life that brought a twinkle to her eyes and a smile on her face.

A convergent palliative care approach to geriatric psychotherapy has been explored for some time now within the medical community, particularly among primary care institutions (Akechi, 2010; Arean and Ayalon, 2005). The blending of Cognitive Behavioral Therapy and Reminiscence Therapy in the treatment of geriatric depression is increasingly becoming a reality and the evidence-based validation of its effective use is consistently showing results.

BIBLIOGRAPHY

Akechi, T. (2010). "Essential Psychological Care in Palliative Medicine." *Psychiatria et Neurologia Japanica,* 112 (10):1029-1035.

Arean, P., Hegel, M., Vannoy, S., Fan, M. Y. & Unutzer, J. (2008). "Effectiveness of Problem-Solving Therapy for Older, Primary Care Patients with Depression: Results from the IMPACT Project," *The Gerontologist,* 48(3), 311-323.

Arean, P., & Ayalon, LO. (2005). "Assessment and Treatment of Depressed Older Adults in Primary Care," *Clinical Psychology: Science and Practice,* 12(3), 321-335.

Ayeers, C. R., Sorrell, J. T., Thorp, S. R., & Wetherell, J. L. (2007). "Evidence-Based Psychological Treatments for Late-Life Anxiety," *Psychology and Aging,* 22(1), 8-17.

Barrowclough, C., King, P.., Colville, J., Russell, E., Burns, A., & Tarrier, N. (2001). "A Randomized Trial of the Effectiveness of Cognitive-Behavioral Therapy and Supportive Counseling for Anxiety Symptoms in Older Adults," *Journal of Consulting & clinical Psychology,* 69(5), 756-762.

Bartels, S. J., Dums, A. R., Oxman, T.E., et al. (2002). "Evidence-Based Practices in Geriatric Mental Health Care: An Overview of Systematic Reviews and Meta-Analyses," *Psychiatric Services* 53(11):1419-1430.

Bohlmeijer, E., Smit, F., Cuijpers, P. (2003). "Effects of Reminiscence and Life Review on Late-Life Depression:

A Meta-Analysis. *International Journal of Geriatric Psychiatry* 18(12):1088-1094.

Cappeliez, P. (2001). "Presentation of Depression and Response to Group Cognitive Therapy with Older Adults," *Journal of Clinical Geropsychology,* 6(3), 165-174.

Chambless, D. L., Hollon, S.D. (1998). "Defining Empirically Supported Therapies," *Journal of Consulting Clinical Psychology* 66(1):7-18.

Chue, K. H. and Chang, T. Y. (2014). "Effectiveness of Group Reminiscence Therapy for Depression Symptoms in Male Veterans: 6-Month Follow-Up." *International Journal of Geriatric Psychiatry.* April, 29(4):377-383.

Connell, P. (1988). "The Effects of Intermittent Reminiscence Therapy on Nursing Home Residents' Depression Levels," (Paper presented at the Annual Meeting of the American Society on Aging (34th, San Diego, CA, March 18-22).

Dempsey, L, Murphy, K., Cooney, A., Casey, D., O'Shea, E., Devane, D., Jordan, F., and Hunter, A. (2014). "Reminiscence in Dementia: A Concept Analysis." *Dementia (London)* March, 13(2):176-92.

Fairman, N., and Irwin, S. A. (2013). "Palliative Care Psychiatry: Update on an Emerging Dimension of Psychiatric Practice." *Current Psychiatry Reports,* July, 15(7):374.

Floyd, M., & Scogin, F. (1998). "Cognitive-Behavior Therapy for Older Adults: How Does it Work?," *Psychotherapy,* 35(4), 459-463.

Francis, J. L. and Kumar, A. (2013). "Psychological Treatment of Late-Life Depression." *Psychiatric Clinics of North America,* Dec, 36(4):561-75.

Gaggioli, A., Scaratti, C., Morganti, L., Stramba-Badiale, M., Agostoni, M., Spatola, C.A., Molinari, E., Cipresso, P., and Riva, G. (2014). "Effectiveness of Group Reminiscence for Improving Wellbeing of Institutionalized Elderly Adults: Study Protocol for a Randomized Controlled Trial." *Trials,* Oct. 25, 15(1):408.

Gallagher-Thompson, D., & Steffen, A. M. (1994). "Comparative Effects of Cognitive-Behavioral and Brief Psychodynamic Psychotherapies for Depressed Family Caregivers," *Journal of Consulting and Clinical Psychology,* 62(3), 543-549.

Gatz, M. (2007). "Commentary on Evidence-Based Psychological Treatments for Older Adults," *Psychology and Aging,* 22(1), 52-55.

Gatz, M., Fiske, A., Fox, L., Kaskie, B., Kasl-Godley, J., & McCallum, T. (1999). "Empirically Validated Psychological Treatments for Older Adults," *Journal of Mental Health and Aging,* 4(1), 9-46.

Gorsuch, Nikki. (1998). "Time's Winged Chariot: Short-Term Psychotherapy in Later Life," *Psychodynamic Counseling,* 4(2), 191-202.

Hallford, D. J., Mellor, D., and Cummins, R. A. (2013). "Adaptive Autobiographical Memory in younger and Older Adults: The Indirect Association of Integrative and Instrumental Reminiscence with Depressive Symptoms." *Memory,* 21(4):444-457.

Herholz, S. C., Herholz, R. S., and Herholz, K. (2013). "Non-Pharmacological Interventions and Neuroplasticity in Early Stage Alzheimer's Disease." *Expert Review of Neurotherapeutics,* Nov., 13(11)1235-1245.

Hinrichsen, G. A. (2008). "Interpersonal Psychotherapy as a Treatment for Depression in Later Life," *Professional Psychology: Research and Practice,* 39(3), 306-312.

Hinrichsen, G. A., & Clougherty, K. F. (2006). *Interpersonal Psychotherapy for Depressed Older Adults.* Washington, D.C.: American Psychological Association.

Hyer, L., Hilton, N., Sacks, A., Freidman, M., & Yeager, C. (2009). "GIST: An Efficient and Effective Cognitive Behavioral Therapy in Long Term Care," *American Journal of Alzheimer's Disease and Other Dementias,* 23 (6), 528-539.

Karel, M. J., Hinrichsen, G. (2000). "Treatment of Depression in Late Life: Psychotherapeutic Interventions," *Clinical Psychology Review* 20(6):707-729.

King, D. A., Heisel, M. J., & Lyness, J. M. (2005). "Assessment and Psychological Treatment of Depression in Older Adults with Terminal or Life-Threatening Illness," *Clinical Psychology: Science & Practice,* 12(3), 339-353.

Klever, S. (2013). "Reminiscence Therapy: Finding Meaning in Memories." *Nursing,* April, 43(4):36-37.

Knight, B. G., & McCallum, T. J. (1998). "Adapting Psychotherapeutic Practice for Older Clients: Implications of the Contextual, Cohort-Based, Maturity, Specific

Challenge Model," *Professional Psychology: Research & Practice,* 29(1), 15-22.

Knight, B. G. & Qualls, S. H. (2006). *Psychotherapy for Depression in Older Adults.* New York: John Wiley & Sons, Inc.

Knight, B. G. (1999). "The Scientific Basis for Psychotherapeutic Interventions with Older Adults: An Overview," *Journal of Clinical Psychology,* 55(8), 927-934.

Laidlaw, K., & Knight, B. (Eds.). (2008). *Handbook of Emotional Disorders in Later Life: Assessment and Treatment.* New York: Oxford University Press.

Landreville, P., Laudry, J., Baillargeon, L., Guerette, A., & Matteau, E. (2001). "Older Adults' Acceptance of Psychological and Pharmacological Treatments for Depression," *Journal of Gerontology: Psychological Sciences,* 56B, 285-291.

Lazar, A., Thompson, H., and Demiris, G. (2014). "A Systematic Review of the Use of Technology for Reminiscence Therapy." Oct., 41(1 Suppl):51S-61S.

Macklin, R., & Arean, P. (2005). "Evidence-Based Psychotherapeutic Interventions for Geriatric Depression," *Psychiatric Clinics of North America,* 28, 805-820.

Meléndez-Moral, J.C., Charco-Ruiz, L., Mayordomo-Rodríguez, T., and Sales-Galán, A. (2013). "Effects of a Reminiscence Program Among Institutionalized Elderly Adults." *Psicothema,* 25(3):319-23.

Morgan, John H. (1987). *From Freud to Frankl: Our Modern Search for Personal Meaning.* Bristol, IN: Wyndham Hall Press.

Morgan, John H. (2010). *Clinical Pastoral Psychotherapy: A Practitioner's Handbook for Ministry Professionals.* South Bend, IN: GTF Books.

Morgan, John H. (2011). "*On Becoming a Person* (1961) Carl Rogers' Celebrated Classic in Memoriam," *Journal of Psychological Issues in Organizational Culture* (II, #3, 95-105).

Morgan, John H. (2012a). "Geriatric Logotherapy: Exploring the Psychotherapeutics of Memory in Treating the Elderly," *Psychological Thought, Vol. 5, #2*, pp. 99-105.

Morgan, John H. (2012b). *Beginning With Freud: The Classical Schools of Psychotherapy* (Expanded 2nd Edition). Lima, OH: Wyndham Hall Press.

Morgan, John H. (2012c). "Geriatric Logotherapy: Exploring the Psychotherapeutics of Memory in Treating the Elderly," *Psychological Thought, Vol. 5, #2*, pp. 99-105.

Morgan, John H. (2012d). "Pastoral Nurture of the Elderly: The 'Happy Memory' in Geriatric Logotherapy" in *Clinical Pastoral Psychotherapy: A Practitioner's Handbook for Ministry Professionals* Expanded 2nd Edition (Mishawaka, IN: GTF Books).

Morgan, John H. (2012e). "Medication and Counseling in Psychiatric Practice: Biogenic Psychopharmacology and Psychogenic Psychotherapy (Partnering in the Treatment of Mental Illness)," in *Clinical*

Pastoral Psychotherapy: A Practitioner's Handbook for Ministry Professionals (Expanded 2nd Edition, Mishawaka, IN: GTF Books).

Morgan, John H. (2013a). "What to Do When There is Nothing to Do: The Psychotherapeutic Value of Meaning Therapy in the Treatment of Late Life Depression," *Health, Culture and Society,* Vol. 5, #1, pp.52-59.

Morgan, John H. (2013b). "Late-Life Depression and the Counseling Agenda: Exploring Geriatric Logotherapy as a Treatment Modality," *International Journal of Psychological Research*, Vol. VI, #1.

Morgan, John H. (2014). *After Freud: The Modern Schools of Psychotherapy* . South Bend, IN: GTF Books.

Morgan, John H. (2015). "The Interpersonal Psychotherapy of Harry Stack Sullivan: Remembering the Legacy," *Journal of Psychology and Psychotherapy* (Volume 5, Issue 1), forthcoming.

Morgan, John H. (2014). "The Deep Structure of Human Nature: Probing the Psycho-Social Propensities in Behavioral Matrices (with special reference to E. O. Wilson)," *Agathos: An International Review of the Humanities and the Social Sciences* (Volume 5 / Issue 2).

Pasacreta, J.V. and Pickett, M. (1998). "Psychosocial Aspects of Palliative Care." *Seminars in Oncology Nursing,* 14 (2):110-120.

Pinquart, M. & Soerense, S. (2001). "How Effective are Psychotherapeutic and Other Psychosocial Interventions with Older Adults? A Meta Analysis," *Journal of Mental Health and Aging, (*72), 207-243.

Powers, D. V. (2008). "Psychotherapy in Long-Term Care: II. Evidence-Based Psychological Treatments and Other Outcome Research," *Professional Psychology: Research and Practice,* 39(3), 257-263.

Rodin, Gary (2013). "Research on Psychological and Social Factors in Palliative Care: An Invited Commentary." *Palliative Medicine,* 27 (10), 925-31.

Satre, D., Knight, B., & David, S. (2006). "Cognitive—Behavioral Interventions with Older Adults: Integrating Clinical and Gerontological Research," *Professional Psychology: Research and Practice,* 37(5), 489-498.

Scogin, F., Welsh, D., Hanson, A., Stump, J., & Coates, A. (2005). "Evidence-Based Psychotherapies for Depression in Older Adults," *Clinical Psychology: Science and Practice,* 12(3), 222-237.

Scogin, F., & McElreath, L. (1994). "Efficacy of Psychosocial Treatments for Geriatric Depression: A Quantitative Review," *Journal of Consulting and Clinical Psychology,* 62(1), 69-74.

Siskin, L. P. (2002). "Cognitive-Behavioral Therapy with Older Adults," *Behavior Therapist,* 25(1), 3-6.

Siskin, L. P. (2002). "Cognitive-Behavioral Therapy with Older Adults," *Behavior Therapist,* 25(1), 3-6.

Stanley, M. A., Wilson, N. L., Novy, D. M., Rhoades, H. M., Wagener, P. D., Greisinger, A. J., & et al. (2009).

"Cognitive Behavior Therapy for Generalized Anxiety Disorder Among Older Adults in Primary Care: A Randomized Clinical Trial," *The Journal of the American Medical Association,* 301(14), 146-1467.

Testad, I., Corbett, A., Aarsland, D., Lexow, K.O., Fossey, J., Woods, B., and Ballard, C. (2014). "The Value of Personalized Psychosocial Interventions to Address Behavioral and Psychological Symptoms in People with Dementia Living in Care Home Settings: A Systematic Review." *International Psychogeriatrics*, July, 26(7):1083-98.

CHAPTER ELEVEN
Retirement and Mental Health: A Decade of Research in Review

Over thirty years ago, Rosen and Palmer (1982) raised the issue of the relationship between professional women's notion of themselves and their attitude towards retirement. The lecture essay is significant at least in terms of its early call for more sophisticated study of this phenomenon which, alas, has yet to be thoroughly studied using evidence-based data. They contended that the psychosocial consequences of this transition had at the time received very little attention (and we might suggest that even today this is a very much under studied correlation). Their empirical studied involved 80 professional women educators in which they discovered that the majority of the interviewees were satisfied with their lives but, they report, a substantial minority suggested periodic restlessness, boredom, and depression. A positive self-concept was evidently credited with a successful adjustment to retirement but factors irrelevant to this successful adjustment included age at retirement, marital status, religious preference, ethnic origin, socioeconomic background, or living alone. Those who reported being dissatisfied with retirement indicated negative and ambivalent feelings and anxiety regarding filling the void in their lives upon retirement. Rosen and Palmer's hypothesis that women's self-concept over a lifetime constitutes the best single predictor of successful adjustment to retirement.

Twenty-five years ago, Pitt (1990) pointed to the conspicuous absence of evidence-based studies linking retirement to mental illness. He did, nevertheless, suggest without evidence that retirement "may contribute a little" to depression, neurosis, subjective anxiety and marital tension. His paper simply raised the question and attempted to scope out the parameters of such a linkage and called for data-base

192

studies of that relationship, suggesting that of all possible responses to the question "denial" was the worst. He then concludes by suggesting a range of "attitudes and activities" which may "promote successful retirement," including "physical and mental activity, good health, adequate means, well considered accommodation, an absorbing interest, congenial company and a philosophy which encompasses morality." The amazing thing about this essay from 25 years ago is that it suggest a trajectory of research which has essentially been followed with evidence-based studies and in-depth longitudinal data-collection all address the very categories of research he suggested back when.

Fletcher and Hansson (1991) used the Social Components of Retirement Anxiety Scale (SCRAS) in a series of four studies involving 308 men and 384 women aged 25 to 76 years for the purpose of assessment retirement anxiety. Among the first of its kind using this research instrument as applied to retirement anxiety, their studies drew from the 23-item SCRAS measures of 4 factors, namely, social integration and identity, social adjustment/hardiness, anticipated social exclusion, and lost friendships. The results of the scale assessment of responses demonstrated a strong prediction of fear of retirement as well as negative attitudes towards it. It failed, however, in its ability to measure a generalized emotional state, demonstrated simply a rather minimal correlation with other more generalized measurements of anxiety and depression. For individuals engaged in major social transitions, elevated scores were recorded particularly as relates to those who were shy, lonely, had fewer instrumental or communal traits, and who expected to have little personal control over their lives after retirement.

Nearly 20 years ago, Sharpley (1997) did the psychological research community a favor by addressing the issue of psychometric properties as relates to self-perceived stress on what was then called the retirement Scale. The

14-item self-report scale called the SSRS (Self-Perceived Stress in Retirement Scale) was used to develop a listing from retiree reports factors which were thought to cause stress in the everyday world of living and working. This listed survey study was then administered to 348 men and 385 women who had recently retired sometime between six months and five years previously. The study found that internal consistency showed high satisfaction levels and that the respondents were sensitive to a range of issues affecting participant stress which, in turn, corresponded with standardized measures of anxiety and depression. This study showed a structure configuration demonstrating three factors of relevance in anxiety and depression induction including missing work, personal health, and relationship issues. Sharpley contended that the effectiveness of the SSRS was demonstrated in this data-base study and proposed its continued and wider ranging use in psychological research on the relationship between stress and retirement.

Kim and Moen (2002) pursued a longitudinal study of the relationship between retirement and post-retirement psychological well-being, a topic of great interest and until their study little investigated with evidence-based data. Using a data-base of 458 married men and women aging 50 to 72 years who were either still working at their primary career employment, just retired, or had already made the transition from employment to retirement within the previous 2 years, Kim and Moen were able to show that the relationship between retirement and psychological well-being necessitated its assessment in terms of the life course context of the retiree. For example, the transition to retirement during the last two years of employment was associated with higher levels of morale among men but being "continuously" retired resulted in a greater degree of depressive symptoms among men. Their studied strongly suggests that understanding the dynamics of the retirement transition as relates to psychological well-being must inevitably be linked to a study of the context within which the retirement transition, including gender, prior level of psychological well-being, spouses' circumstances, and changes in personal control, marital quality, subjective health, and income adequacy) must be considered fundamental factors.

Melzer (2004) and colleagues addressed the wide spread issue of what is considered the common mental disorder prevalence of older men in their 60s based on their assessment of the data gleaned in the National psychiatric Morbidity Survey. Conducted just over ten years ago, the study is still proving to be helpful and provocative in the formulation of questions and conclusions based on data analysis of the NPMS. Their early contention was that, at the time of their studies, there was still a sparsity of studies address the impact which social transitions such as retirement might have upon mental health. From various studies it is commonly known that adverse employment conditions as well as involuntary discharge from employment are directly linked to higher rates of mental disorders, including depression, anxiety, and stress, but Melzer and team suggest that voluntary retirement is associated with the improvement in mental health of the retiree. They set out in this study to attempt an estimation of the prevalence of certain common mental disorders such as stress, anxiety, and depression connected traditional retirement age and in that scenario to identify various factors which might contribute to a better understanding of the differences in rates of occurrence. Using the Methods Data from the 2000 Great Britain's Psychiatric Morbidity Survey which covered 8,580 respondents aged 16-74 years, they focused upon the currently held common mental health disorders (neurotic rather than psychotic) present in the survey pool based on a revised version of the Clinical Interview Schedule. Somewhat unanticipated was the discovery that there was a drastically lower instances of common mental disorders among men between 65 and 69 years as compared to men between 60 and 64 years. This was true for individual disorders evidencing a very high symptoms rate whereas prevalence rates of mental disorders among women peaked at age 50 and declined steadily afterwards with no measurable change in prevalence between ages 60 and 65. Among men, however, there was a high prevalence of common mental disorders who chose to leave work early, i.e., between 50 and 64 years, and only dropping after the traditional retirement age of 65. The only specifically relevant variant in the stabilizing of mental health among retirees had to do with decreased economic hardship of the over 65. The fundamental conclusion from this study by Melzer and team is that within the general population aged 50-74 years, there is a measurable rise in mental health among men after the traditional retirement age of 65 but not among women. However, for men who leave work earlier than the traditional age of 65, prevalence of mental disorders remains somewhat high until the age of 65 when depressive symptoms recede.

Tougas (2004) and colleagues have taken on the commonly held negative view of older workers and their relationship to both identity and relative deprivation as relates to ageism and retirement. They have particularly chosen to address the issue of what leads the aging worker to recognize and acknowledge disparities the older worker and the younger worker. Furthermore, what is the result of the older and aging worker adopting into their own self-image those commonly held characteristics of the older worker. In other words, why do older workers adopt and accept the "older worker" self-image? Tougas and team's focus is particularly upon the connection between personal identity and relative deprivation. The hypothesis was simply states that the more older workers include characteristics of their group into their self-identity and self-image, the more they experience personal deprivation when comparing their own situation to that of younger workers. The research team argued, based on their data-base study of 149 young retirees, that these feelings of diminished self-image and self-identify actually affect the retiree specifically in terms of a lowering of both self-esteem as well as a decline in satisfaction with their life in retirement. Tougas and colleagues confirm their hypothesis by showing that the end-of-career experiences actually do have a direct impact upon the post-retirement life situation of the retiree. They suggest that the more these young retirees integrate characteristics of aging workers, the more they felt actually deprived as compared to their younger co-workers. Self-esteem and the assessment of one's life satisfaction declined markedly as well.

Karpansola (2005) and colleagues addressed themselves to the health problems resulting from depression brought on by early retirement. They chose a cohort of 1,726 Finnish men from 1984 to 2000. Their concern was the reduction in work productivity precipitating early retirement. Depression as baseline (determined by the HPL depression score) constituted the starting point and using pension records provided by the national Pension Registry, Cox's regression analysis was employed to estimate the associations of depression with the risk of all disability pensions, separating out different causes of disability and non-illness based pension. The results were most informative as over 48% of the men studied eventually received disability pensions and 17% of those retired due to mental disorders and 52% of the same retired due to depression. Those in the highest third of depression had a marked increase of risk to non-illness based pensioning, disability pensioning due to mental disorders, chronic somatic diseases, and cardiovascular disease. The mean age for retirement among the cohort with high depression was 57.6 years and low depression was 59.1 years. The results of the study were clear, viz., a high depression score predicted disability due to any cause, especially mental disorders, and non-illness based pensions. Depressed individuals retired on average a year and a half younger than those without depression. Further study is justified in charting the pathways of how mental depression leads worker to seek retirement pension.

Butterworth (2006) and colleagues engaged in a substantial national research project on retirement in Australia, having indicated the sparsity of such evidence-based empirical investigations into a major concern in the national health community. The study was of the mental health problems found among men and women employees during their transition from work to retirement. The interest was in the identifiable relationship between retirement and mental health issues covering a large data base of older adults, factoring in age and known risk factors for mental disorders. From the 1997 National Survey of Mental Health and Well-Being, a cross-sectional survey of 10,641 Australian adults was used. The instances of depression and anxiety disorders was studied using a sub-sample of men (1,928) and women (2,2261) aged 45 to 74 years. The mental health of those studied was assessed using the Composite International Diagnostic Instrument and additional measurements were employed to assess the participants' physical health, demographic and personal characteristics. They found that there was a diminishment of common mental disorders across increasing age groups of both men and women and that women aged 55-59, 65-69, and 70-74 actually had significantly lower rates of mental disorders than those aged 45 to 49. However and in contrast to the women studied, only men aged 65-69 and 70-74 demonstrated any significant lowering of common mental disorders compared to men aged 45 to 49. Furthermore, male retirees were much more likely to have common mental disorders compared to men still employed yet this did not prove to characterized retired men of or nearing the traditional age of retirement at 65. As expected, both men and women suffering from poor health issues were more likely to have diagnosable mental disorders with the findings of this study indicating that for men the relationship between retirement and mental health varies with age but less so with women. Butterworth and team believe that these findings should encouraged weighing mental health issues and their influencing factors when encouraging continued employment among older adults, especially men.

Villamil, Huppert, and Melzer (2006) have produced a really remarkable data-base study linking depression and anxiety to retirement based on a national survey conducted in the United Kingdom. Though it is common knowledge among medical professionals that mental disorders tend to decrease substantially for men at the time of retirement in the United Kingdom, the same is not true for women where there is no significantly measurable decline in mental disorders as women reach retirement age. Willamil and colleagues set out to determine whether or not work status, age or other known risk factors could be held responsible for a reduction in the prevalence of depressive episodes and anxiety disorders at about the time of retirement for both men and women. Based on the 2000 British Psychiatric Morbidity Survey (BPMS) wherein 1,875 men and 2,253 women aged 45 to 75 years were surveyed, the resulting diagnoses were based on the Revised Clinical Interview Schedule (CIS-R). The required adjustments for logistic modeling were made including sociodemographic factors, social network, work status, life events, physical illness as well as disability and the results were informative. Significantly measurable reductions in the prevalence of depression after age 60 for women and 65 for men compared to the youngest age group. Anxiety disorders registered a lower prevalence for men at 80% and for women at 50% and, not surprisingly, work status for men proved significant but not for women.

Szinovacz and Davey (2006) broke new ground on a topic which was beginning to dominate social service agencies, namely, the relationship between depression and grandchild care among retirees. The focus of the study was upon the direct relationship the caring for grandchildren in retirement had upon the development of depressive symptoms among older retirees. The findings in this study showed conclusively that retirement was directly and negatively impacted by the care of grandchildren as related to obligations on well-being as indicated by the rise in depressive symptoms. Retired men, for example, who were free from the care of grandchildren and the attending obligations implied in that relationship showed a high level of a sense of well-being and a low level of anxiety and depression. Women who continued to maintain employment during their older years also were protected against negative effects of extensive grandchild care obligations as relates to a sense of well-being and the absence of depression and anxiety. Szinovacz and Davey's conclusion based on this study suggests that for men the traditional argument that family care obligations spoil the retirement years proved corrected whereas for women that case was not made for such a conclusion but rather to the contrary.

Korkeila (2011) and colleagues set out to study a virtually unstudied classification of workers, namely, employees suffering from personality disorders and the relevance of that classification to retirement issues as compared to anxiety and depression. It proved to be an insightful and provocative investigation. Based on a population of 151,618 employees who had been awarded medical rehabilitations and hospitalizations as determined by standard diagnostic procedures, the cohort was reduced for the study to 1,942 of which 233 were diagnosed with personality disorder, 419 with anxiety disorder, and 1,290 with depression. Hospitalized patients numbered 1,333 of which 354 were diagnosed with personality disorder, 126 with anxiety disorder, and 853 with depression. Of these, early retirement from employment was charted using the National Registry during a five year period with Cox's proportional hazard models used for examining the association of diagnostic groups with risk of early retirement. Adjusting for age, sex, and socioeconomic position, the presumed risk of early retirement for patients with personality disorders was 3.5 fold in rehabilitation and 2.3 fold in hospitalized patients as compared to anxiety disorders. The comparison of early retirement risks for personality disorders versus depression was 1.1 fold which lead Korkeila's research team to conclude that personality disorders increase the risk of early retirement at about the same level as does depression but more than twice that of anxiety disorders.

Bekhet and Azuszniewski (2013) addressed themselves to the issue of cross-cultural differences with respect to the aging process and the adjustments to it with specific interest in a comparative study of the United States and Egypt since both older populations are expected to double by the year 2030. Realizing that with the aging process comes chronic illness increases and many elderly choose or are forced to relocate to retirement communities, Bekhet and Azuszniewski wished to pursue more carefully an evaluation of the positive cognitions and resourceful behaviors of these elderly as relates to adaptive functioning and necessary adjustments to the new living situations precipitated by the aging process. They set out to examine and compare such things as relocation controllability, positive cognitions, resourcefulness and relocation adjustment comparing American and Egyptian older individuals living in retirement communities. Their intent in this cross-cultural comparative study was to increase insight into factors influencing each group which could possibly lead to positive suggestions of how to facilitate the relocation process in both cultures. Factors studied, using a cross-sectional descriptive design research model, including comparing relocation controllability, positive cognitions, resourcefulness and relocation adjustment of a convenience sample of older Americans (n=104) and a convenience sample of older Egyptians (n=94). The specific communities studied were from Northeast Ohio and Alexandria, Egypt. Of the factors studies, only resourcefulness maintained consistency within both groups with older Americans fairing decidedly better in positive cognitions, relocation controllability, and relocation adjustment. The benefit of the study offered a direction for developing positive cognition intervention methods and engaging older individuals in the decision-making process to help their adjustment to relocation. The specific relevance of the study offered suggestions as to how the nursing staff of residential facilities might assist in the positive thinking and resourcefulness training required. These interventions have proven beneficial in reducing stress of relocation by facilitating positive thinking about the inevitability of relocation.

Potocnik and Sonnentag (2013) have conducted a major longitudinal study based on European data of 2,813 retirees as well as 1,372 older employees controlling for health, ageing and retirement in Europe. They were looking at the notion of well-being among older workers and retirees relative to a diversity of activities. Specifically, they examined the impact that engaging in seven different types of activities had upon depression and the quality of life among both retirees as well as older workers over a span of 2 years. They found that such things as volunteering, providing help to others and both going to sporting events and social club activities showed a marked improvement in the quality of life over the 2 year period as reported by the participants. However, there was no measurable impact upon the older employees as opposed to the retirees. An unanticipated finding was that there was a rise in depression among both retirees and older employees who were directly involved in the care of disabled adults. In instances in which retirees were suffering from higher levels of depression, they participation in religious activities resulted in an greater decrease in depression as opposed to those retirees who were suffering at a lower level of depression. An additional finding was that older employees who took active part in political activities experienced a decrease in depression as well.

Chli, Stewart, and Dewey (2013) did a large data-based study of the relationship between variously identified productive activities and the prevalence of depression among a large sampling of older Europeans. The relationship between productive activities and positive health-related and well-being related outcomes which prove favorable is a presumed given, the truth of the matter is this correlation has not consistently been studied or reported upon with any degree of predictability. Chli and colleagues set out to evaluate such a correlation of causal relationship among five productive activities, viz., paid work, formal volunteering, caregiving, informal helping, and caring for grandchildren measurable in a sampling of 7,238 relatively healthy community residents aged 60 years and over in 14 European countries who were suffering from reported depressive symptoms. The research instrument used, viz., the Survey of Health, Ageing and Retirement in Europe, excluded individuals with a history of depression, cognitive impairment, and physical limitations, using the EURO-D assessment instrument to identify depressive symptoms. Not surprising, depression appeared to be less prevalent within individuals who were either employed or self-employed as well as those who participated in formal volunteering and informal helping activities. However, caregiving was rather associated with a higher risk and rate of depression and caring for grandchildren was actually not associated either positively or negatively with the appearance of depression or depressive symptoms. Formal volunteering and caregiving, nevertheless, continued to be associated with depression even after controlling for age, sex, marital status, education, economic status, country and presence of long-term illness. Chli and his team came to the conclusion that participation in formalized volunteering activities may be somewhat important in reducing depression and risks of developing depressive symptoms, nevertheless, caregiving is rather directly associated with a higher risk of depression in older European adults.

Researchers have known for some time that mood disorders are often related to and affected by disturbed sleeping patterns and particularly we know that both depression as well as insomnia often increases the possibility of forced retirement due to disabilities. However and the absence of evidence-based studies of the linkage between insomnia, depression and work-related incapacity leading to pre-mature retirement has yet to be thoroughly researched. Paunio (2014) and colleagues have addressed this void in their research based on the Beck Depression Inventory and its subscale Negative Attitudes Towards Self using 12,063 individual responses to their study focused on sleep quality self-reported with reference to incidences of depression ability retirement symptoms reportedly related to depressive disorders. Their findings included a high percentage (95%) of depression resulting from the onset of poor-quality sleep but with a slight and gradual decline in depression following persistently poor sleep patterns. However and most interesting, among individuals who reported few "recent stressful life events," the emergence of poor sleep resulted in strong instances of depression. Furthermore, the initial appearance of poor sleep patterns increased the danger of disability retirement due to depression as well as those individuals suffering from persistently poor sleep patterns. Paunio (2014) and colleagues concluded from this study that poor sleeping patterns are important data in the etiology of both depression and resulting disability retirement and, they concluded, this information should encourage both early detection as well as treatment of sleep disturbances and poor quality of sleep patterns.

Stancliffe (2014) and colleagues have studied a well-constructed program designed to facilitate the transition from employment to retirement of disabled individuals. The focus of the study was upon the decline in social activities among the retiring disabled worker and the impending probable occurrence of resulting inactivity, social isolation, and loneliness. Using a comparative sampling of men and women averaging 55 years of age who regularly attended a community group once a week, their findings were based on a comparative data-base gathered from first joining a community group and six months later. The data was gathered by trained mentors within the community group itself. There was an 86% retention rate among the participants and the findings included increased involvement in the community group by the studied group who averaged four new social contacts as they gradually reduced their on-the-job working hours. A rise in social satisfaction reported by the study group was noted with the concluding that the use of trained mentors in community social groups is a viable option for developing a retirement lifestyle for individuals with disabilities anticipating retirement.

Airagnes (2014) and colleagues affirm the fact that studies in advance of theirs have consistently show that a positive effect of retirement is manifested in depressive symptoms. That being said, they have directed their attention to the large-scale prospective Gaz et Electricite (GAZEL) cohort to explore whether or not personality itself is a factor in the positive effect of retirement upon depression. Using studies of depression conducted by the Center for Epidemiologic Studies Depression Scale (CES-D) over a number of years including 1993, 1996, 1999, 2002, and 2008 on 9,755 individuals factoring age, gender, occupational grade, history of sickness absences for depression, and alcohol consumption, their attention was focused specifically upon the effect of hostility and type A personality on measurable changes in depression following retirement using a linear model for assessment and analysis. Not surprising but now this evidence-based study validation, they found that higher scores of cognitive and behavioral hostility along with type A personality produced a less improved state of depression following retirement while cognitive hostility remained significant. Participants meeting the clinical depression threshold in the study prior to retirement who were in the lowest cognitive hostility classification were twice as likely to fall short of this threshold after retirement than those in the highest classification. Clearly, Airagnes and colleagues concluded that individual with a high level of cognitive hostility were likely to demonstrate less improvement in depressive symptoms following retirement versus those in the lowest levels of cognitive hostility.

Ladin, Daniels, and Kawachi (20104) have sought to explore position and late-life depression from data provided by 10 European countries with specific attention to socioeconomic inequality arguing that the relevance of higher levels of morbidity and mortality among the poor may have cross-cultural and multi-national evidence, relevance, and representation. Emphasis was place upon the distinction between absolute and relative deprivation in predicting late-life depression as related to both individual and national levels. The large scale data-base of 22,777 men and women (aged 50 – 104 years) from 10 European countries was made available through the Survey of Health, Ageing and Retirement in Europe (SHARE, Wave 1,

Release 2) and the use of multivariate logistic regression within the matrix of relative indexes of inequality. Using the EURO-D scale and corresponding clinical data, late-life depression was measured wherein absolute deprivation was measured using gross domestic product data as well as median household income at the national level and socioeconomic status at the individual level. Discovering a solid north-south gradient in the data, rates of depression ranged from just over 18% in Denmark to nearly 37% in Spain. Ladin and team quite clearly discovered that both absolute and relative deprivation were significant in predicting levels of depression among late-life individuals in both country at the national and individual levels. A key finding, according to the research team, is that the negative impact of social inequality is not surmountable by merely increasing individual or national levels of income and, further, they conclude from their data analysis that increasing in individual levels of income did not have an impact upon the national level of relative deprivation. They have concluded that the disparties in mental health throughout later life where individuals are exposed to higher levels of national inequality experience greater levels of morbidity than those individuals in countries with less inequality. Further research on this disparity between national and individual levels of socioeconomics and its relationship to mental health and particularly depression is called for.

Ghodsbin (2015) and colleagues have explored a fascinating therapeutic approach to the care of elderly people involving what is now more commonly being called "laughter therapy." This evidence-based study was conducted at the Jahandidegan Community Center in Shiraz, Iran, in 2014, involving some 72 seniors over the age of 60. Laughter therapy, a growing modality of treatment in geriatric care and the treatment of depression and creeping dementia, was employed in this study. Using both experimental and control groups, data was collected employing the General Health Questionnaire (GHQ-28) as well as the demographic questionnaire. These 72 senior citizens attended a laughter therapy program consisting of two 90-minute sessions per week over a 6 week period. The statistical findings were somewhat astounding in terms of identifiable correlations between laughter therapy and such things as general health, somatic symptoms, insomnia, and anxiety. In spite of these positive results, there were no measurable correlations between laughter therapy and either social dysfunction or depression. Ghodsbin and colleagues concluded that laughter therapy has proven to have effective benefits in general health among the elderly in spite of its lack of positive impact upon depression.

Lohman (2015) and colleagues set out to determine the correlation between depression among the elderly as relates to various models of frailty and to establish the nature and extent as well as the relevance of the relationship. Some 3,453 participants over the age of 65 were involved in this 2010 Health and Retirement Study and depressive symptoms along with frailty indices from the Centers for Epidemiologic Studies Drepression scale were plotted sorted according to 3 conceptual models, viz., biological syndrome, frailty index, and functional domains and Lohman and his team employed confirmatory factor analysis to identify correlations between depression and the various models of frailty utilized in the CESD scale. The results showed a very high level of significant correlation between each of the three frailty factors and depression – biological syndrome, functional domans, and frailty index. Unquestionably, the study provided evidence-based validation for the significant correlation of frailty and depression in late life suggesting, explained Lohman and colleagues, that psychological vulnerability may very well be a key factor in frailty among the elderly.

Grotz (2015) and colleagues set out to test the relationship, if such exists, between deferred retirement and its relationship to the delaying of the onset of Alzheimer's disease and, it such a correlations does exist, to establish whether or not retirement age can still reliably predict the age at which Alzheimer's disease may set in when two factors are considered, namely, deferred retirement and age onset prediction. A European data-base study of 1,380 Alzheimer's patients, called the Impact of Cholinergic Treatment Use/Data Sharing Alzheimer Cohort (ICTUS/DSA), was used for the gathering of information regarding retirement age, onset of symptoms and covariates. These three factors were gathered as baseline covariates whereas age at diagnosis was rather gleaned from the patient's own medical records before the study actually began. The method used by Grotz and team was a linear mixed model adjusted for gender, education, occupation, center, country, household income, depression and cardiovascular risk factors for the final 815 patients used in this study. The results of the study suggests that there is a measurable relationship between retirement age and the age of the onset of Alzheimer's disease yet there is extreme caution in over valuing these findings owing to selection bias of participants as well as uncertainly in the causality correlates leading the researchers to suggest that further study is mandatory in order to further explicate and validate the relevance of these findings.

Olesen (2015) and colleagues have set out to further explicate a very complex and yet-to-be thoroughly studied relationship between retirement and mental health. They focused their study on 245,082 Danish workers who retired between 2000 and 2006 by examining the prevalence of hospital treatment for depression as compared to the purchase of antidepressant medication before, during, and after retirement. The hypothesis under which they operated was that retirement would be followed by a reduced prevalence of hospital treatment for depression as well as antidepressant purchases after retirement. The Danish National Register provided relevant information on retirement, hospital treatment, and antidepressant purchases for those who participated in the study. Statistical formulas using logistic regression and generalized estimating equations provided data for the yearly prevalence of hospital treatment for depression and antidepressant purchases used in the study cover the time period five years before to five years after retirement. Amazingly, only .2% of the participants were hospitalized with depression in the year of their retirement whereas just over 6% purchased antidepressant medication during the first retirement year. Granted a rise in hospital treatment for depression just prior to and around the retirement year, nevertheless, there was nevertheless a slight decline from 2 years after retirement with a drop in hospitalization. As regards the purchase of antidepressants prior to retirement, there was a levelling off during the retirement year but continued nevertheless. Candidly, Olesen and team concluded that this massive data-based study did not and could not confirm their initial hypothesis that retirement is beneficial for mental health using as a measurement both hospitalization caused by depression and the treatment of depression with antidepressant medication. Olesen and colleagues were only able to suggest that the temporary levelling off of the increase in antidepressant medication treatment at the time of retirement, though possibly suggesting an identifiable benefit, it appears that this benefit was only short lived and further study of this correlation is clearly necessary.

REFERENCES

Airagnes, G; Lemogne, C; Consoli, S.M.; Schuster, J.P.; Zins, M.; and Limosin, F. (2014) "Personality

Moderates the Improvement of Depressive Symptoms After Retirment: Evidence from the GAZEL Cohort," American Journal of Geriatric Psychiatry (Dec. 9:1064-1081).

Bekhet, A.K. and Azuszniewski, J.A. (2013), "Resourcefulness, Positive Cognitions, Relocation Controllability and Relocation Adjustment Among Older People: A Cross-Sectional Study of Cultural Differences," International Journal of Older People Nursing (Vol 8, #3, Sept.:244-252).

Butterworth, P., Gill, S. C., Rodgers, B., Anstey, K. J., Villamil, E., and Melzer, D. (2006), "Retirement and Mental Health: Analysis of the Australian National Survey of Mental Health and Well-Being," Social Science and Medicine (Vol. 62, #5:1179-1191).

Chli, K-S., Stewart, R.; and Dewey, M. (2013), "Participation in Productive Activities and Depression Among Older Europeans: Survey of Health, Ageing and Retirement in Europe (SHARE)," International Journal of Geriatric Psychiatry (Vol. 28, #11: 1157-1165).

Fletcher, W. L. and Hansson, R. O. (1991), "Assessing the Social Components of Retirement Anxiety," Psychological Aging (March, Vol. 6, #1:76-85).

Ghodsbin, F; Sharif Ahmadi, Z; Jahanbin, I.; and Sharif, F. (2015) "The Effects of Laughter Therapy on General Health of Elderly People Referring to Jahandidegan Community Center in Shiraz, Iran, 2014: A Randomized Controlled Trial," International Journal of Community Based Nurse Midwifery (Jan. 3, #1:31-38.

Grotz, C.; Letenneur, L.; Bonsang, E.; Amieva, H.; Meillon, C.; Quertemont, E.; Salmon, E.; Adman, S. (2015)

"Retirement Age and the Age of Onset of Alzheimer's Disease: Results from the ICTUS Study," PLoS One (February 25, Vol. 10, #2).

Karpansalo, M., Kauhanen, J., Lakka, T.A., Manninen, P., Kaplan, G.A., and Salonen, J.T. (2005), "Depression and Early Retirement: Prospective Population Based Study in Middle Aged Men," Journal of Epidemiology and Community Health (Vol. 59, #1:70-74).

Kim, J.E. and Moen, P. (2002), "Retirement Transitions, Gender, and Psychological Well-Being: A Life-Course, Ecological Model," Journal of Gerontological Behavioral Psychological Science and Sociological Science (Vol. 57 May, #3:212-222).

Korkeila, J., Oksanen, T., Virtanen, M., Salo, P., Nabi, H., Pentti, J., Vahtera, J., and Kivimaki, M. (2011), "Early retirement from Work Among Employees with a Diagnosis of Personality Disorder Compared to Anxiety and Depressive Disorders," European Psychiatry (Vol. 26, #1:18-22).

Ladin, Keren; Daniels, Norman; and Kawachi, Ichiro (2014), "Exploring the Relationship Between Absolute and Relative Position and Late-Life Depression: Evidence from10 European Countries," The Gerontologist (Vol. 50, #1:48-59).

Lohman, M; Dumenci, L; and Mezuk, B. (2015) "Depression and Frailty in Late Life: Evidence for a Common Vulnerability," Journal of Gerontological Behavioral Psychology Science and Sociological Science (Jan. 23: 180-186).

Melzer, D., Buxton, J., and Villamil, E. (2004), "Decline in Common Mental Disorder Prevalence in Men During the Sixth Decade of Life: Evidence from the National Psychiatric Morbidity Survey," Social Psychiatry and Psychiatric Epidemiology (Vol. 39, #1: 33-38).

Olesen, K.; Rod,N.H.; Madsen, I.E.; Bonde, J.P.; and Rugulies, R. (2015) "Does Retirement Reduce the Risk of Mental Disorders? A National Registry-linkage Study of Treatment for Mental Disorders Before and After Retirement of 245 082 Danish Residents," Occupational Environmental Medicine (May: 72#5:36-372).

Paunio, T; Korhonen, T; Hublin, C; Partinen, M; Koskenvuo, K; Koskenvuo, M; and Kaprio, J. (2014) "Poor Sleep Predicts Symptoms of Depression and Disabaility Retirement Due to Depression," Journal of Affective Disorders (Oct 14:381-389).

Pitt, B. (1990), "Mental Health in Retirement: Can Deterioration be Prevented?" Journal of Research in Social Health (June, Vol. 110, #3:81-84).

Potocnik, Kristina and Sonnentag, Sabine (2013), "A Longitudinal Study of Well-Being in Older Workers and Retirees: The Role of Engaging in Different Types of Activities," Journal of Occupational and Organizational Psychology (Vol 86, #4:497-521).

Rosen, J. L. and Palmer, M.B. (1982), "Retirement Adaptations and Self-Concept in Professional Women," American Convention of the American Psychological Association (90th, Washington, D.C., August 23-27, 1982).

Sharpley, C.F. (1997), "Psychometric Properties of the Self-Perceived Stress in Retirement Scale," Psychological Report (August, Vol. 81, #1:319-322).

Stancliffe, R.J.; Bigby, C; Balandin, S; Wilson, N.J.; and Craig, D. (2015) "Transition to Retirement and Participation in Mainstream Community Groups Using Active Mentoring: A feasibility and Outcomes Evaluation with a Matched Comparison Group Journal of Intellectual Disability Research (Dec. 11:111-121).

Szinovacz, M.E. and Davey, A. (2006), "Effects of Retirement and Grandchild Care on Depressive Symptoms," International Journal of Aging and Human Development (Vol. 62, #1: 1-20).

Tougas, F; Lagace, M; de la Sablonniere, R.; and Kocum, L. (2004), "A New Approach to the link between Identity and Relative Deprivation in the Perspective of Ageism and Retirement," International Journal of Aging and Human Development (59, #1:1-23).

Villamil, E., Huppert, F. and Melzer, D. (2006), "Low Prevalence of Depression and Anxiety is linked to Statutory Retirement Ages rather than Personal Work Exist: A National Survey," Psychological Medicine (Vol. 36, #7: 999-1009).

CHAPTER TWELVE

Geriatric Narcissism: The Psychotherapeutics of Self-Regard among the Elderly

(a literature review)

A century of research, analysis, and discussion characterizes the study of narcissism based on Freud's pivotal essay, "On Narcissism," in his 1914 *(Zur EinfUHrung Des Narzissmus) Introductory Lectures*, trans. 1917) Part III, Vol. 16, Chapter 26 in which he makes the observation that narcissism is "not necessarily pathological." This, as we know, set off a fire storm of response, challenge, and criticism (Morgan, 2012c). That history, at least for historians of psychoanalysis and more broadly of psychotherapy, is fascinating and needs yet to be comprehensively researched and recorded (Morgan, 2015a). However, that is not our intention here but rather a look back over the last dozen years (2002 – 2014) into the latest developments of research and analysis from the perspective of a variety of competing and complimenting schools of psychotherapy, an enquiry which should prove beneficial in our efforts to re-value the meaning, nature, and function of narcissism.

More specific to our present agenda, we will see to what extent and in what ways such studies have provided a legitimacy to a concept being proposed here, namely, "geriatric narcissism" (Morgan, 2015b). The impetus for this specificity derives from a drift within the popular literature towards a devaluation of the elderly based on a superficial misreading of the nature of "self-regard" and its psychotherapeutic value for geriatric patients (Morgan, 2012d). To have psycho-pathologized such perceived narcissistic behavior among the elderly, particularly those needing home care and institutional care, while serving the marketing needs and aspirations of care-giving institutions, fails in its therapeutic assessment of the need for self-regard among the elderly. The elderly are not so much the consumers of these institutional services but the recipients of those services marketed to their care givers, most commonly family members in search of a management plan too commonly justifying a dismissive attitude toward the elderly in search of self-validation and a sense of self-worth in a declining environment of failing independence (Morgan, 2013).

A brief overview by way of refreshing our understanding of the emergent interest among psychoanalysts and psychotherapists in narcissism (Cheshire, 1983) is in order here. And, of course, we must begin with Freud's pivotal and what has proven over time to be an historic essay (Morgan, 2014a). Though the concept (and the mythological creature bearing its name) dates far back in human history, narcissistic personality disorder as a professionally recognized illness has only been designated such for the last 50 years (Morgan, 2010). Freud's monumental 1914 paper on narcissism constituted the foundational grounds upon which all subsequent research, analysis, and treatment have been based. In that pivotal work, he contended that narcissism is actually a normal part of the human psyche and referred to it as "primary narcissism." As we know, Freud's personality theory was predicated on the notion that individuals are born without a fundamental sense of self and that the ego only emerges with experiential encounters in infancy and childhood. In this matrix, love of one's self could essentially be transferred to others (Morgan, 2014b). The giving and receiving of love, then, becomes crucial to healthy personality development and the diminishment of reciprocity can, according to Freud, lead to a decline in the capacity for self-protection and, alas, the necessity for a narcissistic self-regard becomes crucial for emotional survival.

It was Heinz Kohut (1971) who first introduced the formal concept of "narcissistic personality disorder" in 1968 when he expanded Freud's initial work to include three different types of narcissism, viz., adult, normal, and pathological (Vater, Schroder-Abe, Ritter, Renneberg, Schulze, Bosson, and Roepke, 2013). It took another twelve years before the APA included the disorder in the third edition of the *Diagnostic and Statistical Manual of Mental Disorder* (1980) with specified criteria for identification, diagnosis, and treatment. However, the DSM-5 (2013) removed five of the ten personality disorders which were previously identified, including "narcissistic personality disorder," and a firestorm has been the result ever since. However, since discussions of and, yes, treatment of "narcissistic personality disorder" are apparently here to stay, we might take a moment to refresh our minds regarding its fundamental characteristics as originally identified and then move to a careful assessment of the last dozen years of diagnosis and treatment relative to geriatric psychotherapy. As we will subsequently see, geriatric narcissism may actually prove to be nothing more than an elevated self-protective sense of self-regard among the elderly who too often find themselves dismissed and overlooked by both their care givers and the social matrix of relationships in which they find themselves vulnerable.

The suggestion made by practicing professionals in psychotherapy is that since narcissistic personality disorder is characterized by self-centeredness, lack of empathy, and an exaggerated sense of self-importance, it necessarily has a negative impact upon a full spectrum of life including social, family, and work relationships. Furthermore, individuals with narcissistic personalities are commonly seen as arrogant, confident, and self-centered but when diagnosed as a "disorder," these individuals have exaggerated manifestations of these same personality characteristics. With only about 1 percent of adult Americans affected by this perceived disorder, it is considerably less common and much less likely to be diagnosed and treated than more common personality disorders such as borderline personality disorder, antisocial personality disorder, or histrionic personality disorder.

With its disappearance from the DSM-Vin 2013, its diagnosis and treatment is very much uncertain at this point. The illusive nature of these characteristics – when are they commonly accepted forms of behavior and when have they become evidence of an illness or a disorder is the question – are evidenced in the DSM-IV listing of symptoms which, clearly, lead the APA in DSM-V to suspend this classification of behavior as a personality disorder. Symptoms listed were: (1) An exaggerated sense of one's own abilities and achievements, (2) A constant need for attention, affirmation and praise, (3) A belief that he or she is unique or "special" and should only associate with other people of the same status, (4) Persistent fantasies about attaining success and power, (5) Exploiting other people for personal gain, (6) A sense of entitlement and expectation of special treatment, (7) A preoccupation with power or success, (8) Feeling envious of others, or believing that others are envious of him or her, and (9) A lack of empathy for others.

Etiology and causality of this perceived disorder were always in dispute but there is a general professional consensus that such things as the childhood experience of parental overindulgence, excessive praise, unreliable parenting, and a lack of realistic responses to life situations constitute a matrix contributing to the emergence of this disorder. Clearly, there is a consensus among psychotherapists that individuals with narcissistic personality disorder are commonly characterized as appearing to be arrogant, conceited, self-centered, and haughty. I say "perceived to be" for professionals are beginning to reassess these characteristics relative to the older adult in light of a new movement towards validating this matrix of behaviors within the context of geriatric self-regard rather than narcissism. Traditionally, narcissistic persons were perceived to imagine themselves superior to others, occupied with successful lifestyle symbols such as cars and clothes, but in spite of this exaggerated sense of self-importance, they frequently are solicitous of praise and attention and extremely sensitive to negative criticism and personal attacks. One of the factors in the APA's decision to drop narcissistic personality disorder from the DSM-V had to do with the illusive nature of treatment for an increasingly ill-defined disorder. Since psychotropic medication proved problematic in terms of diagnosis and treatment of amorphous behavioral composites, psychotherapy made an attempt to offer a diagnostic and treatment plan but owing, again, to its illusive character and since usually treatment was sought not by the patient but by the family or caregivers, again there proved to be a consistent failure in treatment.

Given that narcissistic behavior has now been called into question as a legitimate personality disorder and in light of our interest here in what I have chosen to call "geriatric narcissism" with its potential for positive self-regard, it might prove helpful to follow the development over the past dozen years of researchers working on this topic. By doing so, it is possible that we might vindicate the phenomenon of geriatric narcissism from the designation as a "personality disorder" to a more positively descriptive designation as a "personality characteristic" of elderly persons facing an increasingly dismissive caregiving environment practiced by both family members and the care-giving professionals. What has been called geriatric narcissism might, then, be more correctly labeled "geriatric self-regard under stress." Let us explore the recent research literature from the past decade beginning with the pivotal study of Stucke and Sporer in 2002 and end with the 2014 essay by Furnham and Crump, making it a full century since Freud's 1914 essay "On Narcissism."

A decade ago and well in advance of the APA's decision to drop "narcissistic personality disorder" from the DSM-V, Stucke and Sporer (2002) gave a careful assessment of the Baumeister, Smart, and Boden studies of "self-concept clarity" among university undergraduates. Though numerically a small study and of young adults rather than older, the findings constituted an early evidence-based study of the disorder based on an examination of selected predictors of anger, depression, and verbal aggression brought on by an ego threat based on false performance feedback from an intelligence text. A sub-set agenda was an examination of the mediating effects of the various participants' "negative emotions" as a further extrapolation of the aggressive reactions to intelligence text failures. As anticipated, the joint studies demonstrated that both narcissism and self-concept clarity were clearly predictors of negative emotions and aggressive behavior following the induced failure of the participants. The conclusions based on the evidence was that what were assessed as "high narcissists" with a "low self-concept" responded to the results of the test with anger and aggression upon notification of failure but the less narcissistic participants with a measurable "high self-concept" responded with depression rather than anger. A further evidence-based conclusion was that the anger and aggression shown by the low self-concept participants was directed at the ego-threatening feedback rather than towards oneself and, furthermore, both the anger and the depression were predictors of the aggressive response following notification of failure but, nevertheless, they did not "mediate the relation between narcissism, self-concept, performance feedback, or aggression."

The following year (2003), Twenge and Campell analyzed four related studies of narcissistic versus non-narcissistic individuals with respect to the relatedness of social rejection to manifestations of anger and aggression. Again, as with the Strucke and Sporer (2002) study, Twenge and Campell struggled with an operational definition of "narcissistic personality disorder" and the perimeters of its application. Indications of anger and aggression posed no problem in their assessment of a behavioral matrix, but the differentiation of the individuals designated "narcissistic" versus "non-narcissistic" proved challenging. The first of four studies relied upon self-reported past episodes of social rejection on the part of the respondents in which Twenge and Campbell correlated positively narcissism with feelings of anger whereas narcissism was correlated negatively with rather internalized negative emotions. Through an operational lab manipulation construct of social rejection, replication of these findings were validated and, furthermore, they found that individuals labeled narcissistic were clearly more aggressive towards persons who rejected them (called "direct aggression") as well as more aggressive (called "displaced aggression") towards innocent third party individuals when experiencing social rejection. The relevance of these findings to geriatric narcissism and older adult depression and self-regard studies is clearly evident. Following social acceptance, however, individuals designated narcissistic were not more aggressive than non-narcissistic individuals. Twenge and Campell suggested that self-esteem is relatively insignificant in predicting aggressive behavior in response to social rejection on the part of narcissistic individuals and, therefore, they conclude that a combination of narcissism and social rejection clearly is a predictor of aggressive behavior.

In 2004, Altmeyer took a closer look at the relationship of the self, narcissism, and inter-subjectivity in psychoanalytic theory as relates to conceptual development.

The significance of this paper was its historical overview of both the theoretical and professional development and challenges faced by psychoanalysis within the framework of a rise in a multiplicity of psychotherapeutic assessment and treatment options within the counseling profession. Owing to Altmeyer's own training and theoretical orientation, the essay concentrated its attention upon the relationship between theory and clinical practice within the psychoanalytic school of professionalism, emphasizing that school's approach to the study and treatment of narcissism and the narcissistic personality disorder versus other psychotherapeutic theories of treatment not based on psychoanalytic theory. The focus was upon the intersubjective processes inherent within psychoanalytic analysis and treatment. Altmeyer (2004) is eager to emphasize that narcissism itself (as understood by Freud and the Freudian school) and inter-subjectivity are not implicitly contradictory psychological features and that an inter-subjective definition of narcissism must be developed and elaborated upon with the historical context of Freud's initial theoretical explication of this behavioral matrix including both his philosophical approach to an individual's inter-subjective experience as well as empirical evidence found in the research data of infant behavior. This article served as a major reminder to the psychological community of the contribution of Freud's early investigation of narcissism and the relevance of his analysis.

Coming out of these early studies in 2002, 2003, and 2004, there was a growing dissatisfaction with the meagerness of empirical data and evidential treatment findings as relates to narcissism generally and the narcissistic personality disorder of the DSM specifically. Responding to that growing discontent was the essay by Kubarych, Deary, and Austin (2004). In keeping with this paradigm shift towards evidence-based empirical studies allowing for the quantification of findings such that HMOs and insurance companies would have documentation on "treatment plans and success," the emergence of Aaron Beck's CBT documentation surveys set the stage for a whole new movement towards quantifiability of psychological research. The Narcissistic Personality Inventory (NPI) is, for example, the most widely used measurement instrument in the study of narcissism. In Kubarych, Deary, and Austin's 2004 study, they had 338 undergraduates complete the NPI in addition to a battery of personality questionnaires which included the NEO-FFI (Neuroticism, Extraversion, Openness, Agreeableness, and Conscientiousness-Five Factor Inventory) as well. They found weaknesses and inconclusive non-sequitorial results when looking at the exploratory principal components analysis which actually indicated that the NPI (as it had been developed at the time) had both a two and even three-factor structural character and that confirmatory factor analyses were applied to one, two, and three-factor models in the research instrument. Because the fit indices were judged poor but typical of models involving multiple item-level variables, they found that the fits could be somewhat enhanced by permitting "plausible correlated error terms" in cases involving similar content items. By and large, they explain, the NPI as used here was designed to measure general narcissistic constructs consisting of two or three separate correlated factors such as power, exhibitionism, and what they chose to classify as "being a special person," or more commonly labelled "personal exceptionalism." While proposing a psychometrically improved NPI using these findings as a guide, they suggested that in its present form confirmatory factor analysis was able to produce some insights which were not otherwise evidenced in their exploratory factor analysis. Theses researchers observed that the NEO correlations (a factor of 0.36) for both extraversion and low agreeableness except when related to the highly significant correlations for low neuroticism and high openness to experience were of little value or significance.

Lest it be forgotten who began this conversation early in the century, Crockatt (2006) offered to revisit the classic text of Freud, "On Narcissism: An Introduction," just by way of refreshing our memory of his insightful salvo into then unchartered territory. This essay caused a stir within the psychological community for those who knew Freud's work and valued it as well as for those who did not and preferred not to know. To understand the essay on narcissism, Crockatt explained, one must first understand the historical context within which psychoanalysis evolved as a therapeutic treatment and a matrix of interrelated theories of personality development. This could only be done by following Freud's own personal history of development from medical school training to the emergence of psychoanalysis as a system of analysis and treatment. Following this historical contextualization of Freudian psychoanalysis, Crockatt commenced a carefully constructed exegesis of the essay itself, a splendidly executed recitation of Freud's work on narcissism including his own commentary and critique of Freud's insights and suggestions regarding the concept. Three particular applications of Freud's analysis were considered, viz., homosexuality, hypochondria, and psychosis and Crockatt concludes with references to Klein and post-Kleinian developments in narcissistic theories from the psychoanalytic perspective.

The study of ego threat's relationship to anger and aggression conducted by Bond, Ruaro and Wingrove (2006) was recognized at the time within the profession as a major contribution to this matrix. When pursuing a study of narcissism, taking into account the ego, anger, and aggressive behavior, it has proven crucial to clarity of assessment and treatment. This study provided early on just such a matrix analysis and a sequencing of key variables affecting a diagnosis of narcissism. They began with a domain assumption that ego threat to an individual constitutes a potential precipitator of both anger and aggression. Such an assumption is most characteristic when applied to geriatric narcissism. They proposed that anger, in such instances, may function as a defense mechanism against emotional unpleasantness and, as a consequence, the recognition of an individual's vulnerability should result in the reduction of anger and aggressive behavior. Using a data-base study, participants were randomly assigned one of three classification, viz., anger expression, vulnerability expression, or distraction conditions. They were presented twice with four different scenarios in which ego-threatening situations were described and after the first presentation, each participant was asked to rate their own feelings of anger and, after the second presentation, they were asked to write down their feelings within the context of their previously assigned condition and then were asked again to rate the level of their assessed anger. Completing the reading reaction time task assessing their aggressiveness, they then rated themselves on such traits as narcissism, anger, and self-concept clarity. As anticipated, all participants, after reading the story, became angry and stayed angry even after anger expressive behavior but such behavior was reduced after vulnerability expression and distraction were alleviated. Their findings suggested that individuals with an angry disposition expressed an increase in aggression after having been given an opportunity to express their anger. This "trait anger" was able to predict angry moods, both pre- and post- task, as well as poor self-concept clarity and aggression. These researchers concluded that narcissism was associated with angry moods following the ego-threatening stories and, therefore, the recognition of vulnerability in ego-threatening situations necessarily led to correct mood labeling. This, they contended, offered a positive benefit to healthy assessment of ego-threatening responsive behavior and the vindication of narcissism as not necessarily a negative factor in self-regard defense mechanisms. This study greatly enhanced the positive use of the concept of "geriatric self-regard" as more descriptively indicative of what has otherwise here been called "geriatric narcissism."

Granted both the complexity of defining narcissism sufficiently precise as to secure the assent of the psychological profession's approval as well as in light of the DSM's discontinuance of the label narcissistic personality disorder, Horvath and Morf (2009) have presented a two-sequenced study of non-clinical individuals assessed as narcissistic designed to identify a behavioral matrix for the protection of one's self-esteem. This behavioral matrix is thought to serve as a protective mechanism against ego-threats and serves to foster what they characterize in these studies as "a grandiose sense of self." Their work is a classic illustration of the effective use of key assessment instruments such as the LDT (Lexical Decision Task) used in combination with the sequential subliminal priming task and, in addition, they also used the NPI (Narcissistic Personality Inventory), the RSES (Rosenberg Self-Esteem Scale), and specifically for depression the BDI (Beck Depression Inventory). In the first study, they used the LDT in combination with the sequential subliminal priming task and in the second study they employed what was characterized as "instructed thought suppression" in an effort to establish the existence, or not, of defense strategies which were consciously and intentionally designed to suppress feelings of worthlessness or at least subconsciously repress such feelings during the use of the LDT task. Individuals involved in both studies were asked to complete measurements of narcissism as determined by the NPI, self-esteem as measured by the RSES, and depression as measured by the BDI. Their findings suggested that narcissistic individuals more often than not have specific defense mechanisms in place which include both hypervigilance and increased sensitivity when it comes to identifying ego threats and, as a result, they found that initial feelings of worthlessness are rather quickly stifled through the use of automatic repressive behavior, thereby assisting the narcissistic individual in the protection and defense of their grandiose self-perceptions.

While understandably immersed in daily practice of psychotherapy, it is helpful occasionally for professional practitioners to be both reminded of the historical roots of their profession and to have pointed out the contextualization of their theory-based assessments and diagnoses. Hartmann (2009) has done us all a big favor by doing just that in this fascinating discussion of the historical origins of the concept of narcissism and specifically its relatedness to the emergence of self psychology. Psychoanalysis has given us the original description of narcissism, thanks to Freud, and its checkered history and current status of ambiguity must not be overlooked or taken for granted. Hartmann gives a brief but poignant history of narcissism and its definitional relatedness to what is now popularly called self psychology with special reference to Honneth's (1995) concept of "struggle for recognition," a concept based on self-object experiences. What makes Hartmann's treatment here so helpful is his thorough discussion of the various schools of thought concerning the treatment of narcissism with special attention to the psychoanalytic tradition in Europe. Kohut's (1971) use of the concept of self and its relationship to self-objects is shown by Hartmann to be relevant to any discussion of narcissism. And, he explains, since self psychology is sometimes thought of as a sub-set of developmental theory, attachment research applicable to mentalization is brought into the discussion. Self psychology's use of inter-subjectivity is then connected in Hartmann's treatment to systems theory. He explains that since "empathy" as a relevant term in any discussion of narcissism must be understood as a contagion on which cognitive cortical processes are necessarily over-laid, developed theories of empathy involving neurobiological research further suggests the central role of empathy. Based on this historico-theoretical discussion of narcissism, he then proceeds to emphasize the therapeutic role in psychoanalytic self psychology which presumes a disruption and reconstruction process by means of reconstituting internationalization which occurs in the interaction between patient and psychotherapist. The overall assessment of this massive piece of history and theory, Hartmann suggests, calls into focus a rising concern for a more intentional holistic approach to the treatment of narcissism. Certainly this is relevant in the use of the concept of "empathy" as relates to geriatric narcissism and the experience of self-regard among older adults.

Though narcissism and depression have, over the years since Freud's 1914 essay "On Narcissism," been linked by both psychoanalysts and phenomenologists working in these two pathologies, there has until now been an awkward void in empirical evidence for such a link. Tritt, Ryder Ring, and Pincus (2010) set out to establish whether or not such a link existed and, if so, could they provide an evidence-based study validating that linkage. It is generally understood within counseling circles that a common characteristic of narcissism is that of the grandiose behavioral matrix with both adaptive and maladaptive features rather than those common to the depressive state such as vulnerability traits. These researchers set out to assess the relationship between narcissistic personality and the depressive temperament using a recently developed and highly approved measurement instrument to determine a wide range of pathological narcissistic traits. They further, and as an aside to the point of this study, analyzed several distinctive behavioral manifestations involved in linking depressive temperament and pathological narcissism affecting other temperaments. In this study, they used commonly employed and very successful research instruments including the Pathological Narcissism Inventory, the Temperament Evaluation of the Memphis, Pisa, Paris, and San Diego Auto-questionnaire (TEMPS-A), and a somewhat modified Schedule of Fatigue and Anergia (SOFA). A data-base of 228 participants in the study produced these results, viz., they found that Component 1 items reflected a narcissistic vulnerability-negative affect when narcissistic needs were not met by the respondents whereas Component 2 items reflected a narcissistic grandiosity-positive affect related to self-enhancement. Consequently, Tritt and colleagues concluded that Component 1 significantly predicted depressive traits even after controlling for Component 2 temperaments. The final conclusion, granted the limited nature of their study owing to its homogenous, non-clinical sample unscreened for clinical depression and its reliance upon self-report questionnaires, led them to argue that depressive traits are associated with narcissistic disturbance when narcissistic injury is sought to be avoided. This, they conclude, might prove informative and helpful in the psychotherapeutic treatment of depression by taking full account of narcissistic tendencies. Its value in assessing depression within geriatric narcissistic individuals was emphasized.

The strength of Horvath and Morf's (2010) research on the relationship between narcissism and self-esteem was greatly enhanced by their study replication, a research method which is increasingly being called for in behavioral science research in emulation of the physical and biological sciences. Replication constitutes evidence-based research to a higher level and Horvath and Morf have used it in their 2010 study 1 and study 2 projects focusing upon a distinction they sought to validate between "being grandiose" and "feeling worthless." Their sequences Study

1 and 2 examined the manner in which narcissism and self-esteem were predictors of self-ratings and processing of worthlessness and grandiosity. The Study 1 took a close look at the self-view of narcissists and other individuals who registered a high self-esteem who were asked to evaluate the self-descriptiveness of worthlessness and grandiosity. The Study 2 replicated that process using a different sampling base who were furthermore asked to remember half of the items examined while forgetting the other half. The Rosenberg Self-Esteem Scale and the Narcissistic Personality Inventory were used to measure both the self-esteem and narcissistic responses. Their findings verified their original hypothesis that the self-enhancement among narcissists is evidenced mostly in Milgram's agentic domains such as self-directed activities aimed at personal development or personally chosen goals, whereas individuals with a measurable high self-esteem quotient find self-enhancement when in communal groups. Whereas the narcissistic person bragged about their grandiosity, the high self-esteem individual was measurably more modest. Genuine self-esteem and narcissism, it was concluded, both pose different self-goals which eventuate in differing self-regulation strategies.

Though studies of narcissism have been rather popular since Freud's initial salvo into the topic in 1914, most of these studies have concentrated on either children and adolescents or young to middle-aged adults. During the past 20 years, the number of studies of narcissism directed specifically and solely to the elderly number less than a dozen. Balsis, Eaton, Cooper, and Oltmanns (2011) chose to address this void in data-based research in what has become a pivotal paper on the topic. Their interest in personality disorders generally among the elderly and, in this case, that of narcissistic personality disorder (NDP), is the result of the generally held belief among psychotherapists that NPD diminishes with age, or at least "softens." However, as they began to discover in this study, recent empirical evidence, as well as a plethora of anecdotal papers, have suggested that this is not actually true, but rather personality disorders generally and narcissistic personality disorder specifically are more commonly characteristic of the elderly than generally presumed and that these disorders have specific characteristics precipitated by the aging process itself. They are critical of the DSM-IV personality disorder criteria as too ready to overlook these uniquely age-relevant characteristics owing, they suggest, to the insufficient understanding of the relevance of the aging process to personality development. Therefore, without age-appropriate criteria at the disposal of the psychotherapist or clinician, these professions working with the elderly are too commonly unable to measure personality disorders with sufficient precision. They contend that such deficiency can easily be alleviated through the use of a better understanding of older adults by the development and use of a more solidly based empirical and clinical description of symptoms and related behavioral matrices drawn from the effective use of refined research instruments which are now readily available. They demonstrated the effectiveness of this approach in a case study of an elderly female suffering from narcissistic personality disorder and showed that such an approach is relevant by demonstrating that narcissistic personality disorder does, indeed, impair functioning in several identifiable ways.

Beginning with a generalization that narcissistic personalities are inclined to pursue a self-oriented superiority and status even when the cost negatively impacts personal relationships, Balsis and team set out to demonstrate evidence-based findings suggesting that "social comparisons" are a key ingredient in this behavioral matrix. They further suggest that this tendency to social comparisons, when carefully observed and measured, should serve to differentiate narcissistic personality disorder from individual healthy self-esteem. Though these domain assumptions are rather commonly held within the counseling professions, Krizan and Bushmann (2011) intended in their study to demonstrate the correctness of these observations using an empirical study based on a test examining individual differences observed and measured in everyday comparison activities. They concluded that individuals diagnosed as narcissists, as compared to healthy high self-esteem individuals, (1) were more inclined to make frequent socially downward comparisions, (2) tended to think of themselves as rather better-off than individuals they defined as important persons in their social matrix, and (3) were inclined to think of themselves as rather superior to those same individuals. Furthermore, they concluded that these narcissistic individuals' positive emotional reactions to such self-flattering comparisons tended to be based upon their own personally high self-esteem leading Krizan and Bushmann to conclude that such comparison behavior does, indeed, play a central role in the persistent pursuit of status and admiration among narcissists.

For purposes of argument, Egan and Lewis (2011) began by embracing a presumed truism that such behavioral characteristics as shame, narcissism, and self-esteem are the product of a personal ego threat resulting from provocative, frustrated, and self-reported aggressive behavior. Employing the five-factor model of openness, conscientiousness, extraversion, agreeableness, and neuroticism as a measuring device for these three variables, Egan and Lewis (2011) sought to determine their actual influence upon aggression. Using a data-based study of 150 individuals, they were unable to establish validation for an integrated ego threat construct based on the components of this concept. They found that whereas shame, provocation, and frustration were loaded with hostility affecting an aggression feature, anger as well as verbal and physical aggression based on the Narcissistic Personality Inventory scale produced a rather easily identifiable narcissistic aggression dimension. Therefore, they concluded, self-esteem did not actually relate to either factor whereas path analysis did reveal that affective aggression was able to predict neuroticism while narcissistic aggression was reinforced by low agreeableness, extraversion, and masculinity. Finally, they were able to demonstrate effectively that ego psychology models have a tendency to exaggerate emotion's influence on expressive aggression.

Though not specifically applied to older adults, Meier and Semmer (2012) have produced a most fascinating and relevant study precisely to our concerns regarding self-regard and the elderly which too often has a tendency to be described as geriatric narcissism. They took a close empirical look at the role of narcissism as it affects the relationship between a lack of reciprocity, defined as "feeling under-benefited," and irritation in the workplace among employees. Embracing for purposes of the study the commonly held opinion among professional counselors that the narcissistic personality has a strong tendency towards an inflated self-view and a sense of entitlement, Meier and Semmer ventured to propose that in the absence of a sense or experience of reciprocity, there would be an identifiably measurable sense of irritation suggesting an impaired sense of well-being on the part of the individual employee and that, therefore, the predicted response to this evidential lack of reciprocity for those measuring high on the scale of narcissism would inevitably be stronger than those judged non-narcissistic. These hypotheses were carefully examined using two large cross-sectional samples – the first being of 106 air force pilots, and the second being of 103 employees in various organizations. The data was gleaned using both the Narcissistic Personality Inventory (NPI) and variously created scales assessing both the absence of reciprocity as well as irritation in which a lack of reciprocity was positively related to irritation. As anticipated but now empirically verified, the relationship between reciprocity and irritation was measurably higher among individuals assessed as strongly narcissistic versus a much lower relationship between reciprocity and irritation among those assessed as not narcissistic.

Amidst the swirling discussions precipitated by the APA's leaks that narcissistic personality disorder was being scrutinized for possible exclusion from the DSM-V, many researchers launched into a frenzy of data-based study of narcissism in all of its varied forms. Kubarych, Deary, and Austin (2013) entered the fray by revisiting the utility of the Narcissistic Personality Inventory which, up until this DSM-V *brouhaha*, had been used primarily for the purpose of assessing sub-clinical narcissism as applied to pathological narcissism in patients with narcissistic personality disorder (NPD). Their data-based study focuses upon an extreme-group approach in which 52 NPD patients along with 44 healthy control individuals had their narcissism scores compared. Using the Rosenberg Self-Esteem Scale, the question of whether or not explicit self-esteem was suppressed between the interaction of group membership and identified NPI narcissism was examined. Furthermore, general psychological impairment was evaluated using the Symptomchecklist (SCL-90-R) as well as that of depression using the Beck-Depressions-Inventor (BDI-I). Narcissistic personality disorder patients, it was found, actually did not score higher on the NPI when compared to healthy control individuals but, however, as expected, the NPD patients did score much higher on the narcissism subscale using the Dimensional Assessment of Personality Pathology-Basic Questionnaire (DAPP-BQ). Indirect effects, it was found, showed a suppression of NPI scores by NPD patients based on their low self-esteem. The conclusion, according to Kubarych, Deary, and Austin, was drawn that the NPI does not effectively function as a valid indicator of NPD unless there is an explicit control for self-esteem among narcissistic patients. Their empirical refinement of the relationship between NPD and NPI has made this a key study in the field of narcissism.

Daring to embrace Freud's 1914 notion of the validity of a distinction between pathological and normal narcissism (a distinction the profession since Freud has been reluctant to either employ or explore), Roche, Pincus, Lukowitsky, Menard, and Conroy (2013) took up the challenge and have made a major contribution with their recent exploratory study of the distinction. They began with the observation that research into narcissistic personality disorder has suffered from a lack of clarity in the distinction between normal and pathological descriptions of narcissism owing to the poor quality of calibration of narcissistic behavioral matrices. They proceeded to articulate the distinction and then progressed to a high level attempt at actually integrating both types of narcissism as defined by Freud into a single model for analysis which was centered round self-regulating mechanisms. Offering both theoretical and empirical evidence for this endeavor, they attempted to demonstrate how, by modeling pathological and normal narcissism as a two-dimensional phenomenon, narcissistic behavior can find a method of resolving many of the inconsistencies in narcissistic research particularly as involved in assessing adaptive and maladaptive behavioral expressions of narcissism.

From Stucke and Sporer's 2002 landmark study to Roche, Pincus, Lukowitsky, Menard, and Conroy's 2013 efforts at reintegrating research on narcissism, both pathological and normal, constitutes a decade of incrementally advancing sophistication in the discussion of both the narcissistic personality disorder and the relevance of discussions of narcissism within the context of a massive growth in geriatric psychotherapeutic study and research (Morgan, 2012b). It has been a century since Freud's "On Narcissism" essay appeared as a focus and topic of research and discussion within the psychoanalytic community and the last decade has moved away from the APA's disinclination to further perpetuate NPD as a personality disorder. What has been suggested in this essay by way of a review of the pivotal research over the past dozen years is the serious need for a sustained inquiry into the meaning and relevance of narcissistic behavioral research in its application to the study of older adults and the elderly (Egan, Chan, Shorter, Veselka, and Vernon, 2014). As these studies have shown both directly and indirectly, a legitimation and validation of self-regard, once passed off as merely narcissistic behavior of the elderly (Morgan, 2012a), among older persons is a proper response to the social and psychological milieu within which the elderly often find themselves situated. Clearly, more research is needed in what must be thought of as a positive form of geriatric narcissism.

REFERENCES

Altmeyer, M. (2004). "Self, Narcissism, and Intersubjectivity," *Selbstpsychologie* 5(3-4): 275-288.

American Psychiatric Association (2000). "Narcissistic Personality Disorder." *Diagnostic and Statistical Manual of Mental Disorders,* 4th Edition (DSM-IV-TR).

Balsis, S., Eaton, N., Cooper, L., and Oltmanns, T. (2011). "The Presentation of Narcissistic Personality Disorder in an Octogenarian: Converging Evidence from Multiple Sources," *Clinical Gerontology*, 34(1):71-87.

Baumeister, R., Smart, L., and Boden, J. (1996). "Relation of Threatened Egotism to Violence and

Aggression: The Dark Side of High Esteem," *Journal of Personality and Social Psychology,* 103 (1), 5-33.

Bond, A. J., Ruaro, L., Wingrove, J. (2006). "Reducing Anger Induced by Ego Threat: Use of Vulnerability Expression and Influence of Trait Characteristics," *Personality and Individual Differences,* 40(6): 1087-1097.

Cheshire, Neil M. (1983). "Narcissism" in the *Encyclopedic Dictionary of Psychology* edited by Rom Harre and Roger Lamb (Cambridge, MA: The MIT Press).

Crockatt, P. (2006). "Freud's 'On Narcissism: An Introduction,'" *Journal of Child Psychotherapy,* 32(1):4-20.

Egan, V., Lewis, M. (2011). "Neuroticism and Agreeableness Differentiate Emotional and Narcissistic Expressions of Aggression," *Personality and Individual Differences,* 50(6): 845-850.

Egan, V., Chan, S., Shorter, G.W., Veselka, L., Vernon, P. A. (2014). "The Dark Triad: Happiness and Subjective Well-being," *Personality and Individual Differences,* 67(1): 17-22.

Flanaga, L. M. (1996). "TheTheory of Self Psychology," in (eds.) Berzoff, J., Flanagan, l.M., & Hertz, P. *Inside Out and Outside In* (New Jersey: Ason Aronson, Inc.

Freud, Sigmund (1914), "On Narcissism," *Zur EinfUHrung Des Narzissmus (Introductory Lectures,* trans. 1917), Part III, Vol. 16, Chapter 26.

Kohut, Heinz (1971). *The Analysis of the Self* (New York: International University Press).

Furnham, A., Crump, J. (2014). "A Big Five Facet Analysis of Sub-Clinical Narcissism: Understanding Boldness in Terms of Well-Known Personality Traits," *Personality and Mental Health,* 8(3): 209-217.

Hartmann, H-P. (2009). "Psychoanalytic Self Psychology and Its Conceptual Development in Light of Developmental Psychology, Attachment Theory, and Neuroscience," *Annals of the New York Academy of Sciences,* 1159, 86-105.

Honneth, Axel (1995). *The Struggle for Recognition: The Moral Grammar of Social Conflicts* (N.Y.: Polity Press).

Horvath, S., Morf, C. C. (2009). "Narcissistic Defensiveness: Hypervigilance and Avoidance of Worthlessness," *Journal of Experimental Social Psychology,* 45(6): 1252-1258.

Horvath, S., Morf, C. C. (2010). "To Be Grandiose or Not to be Worthless: Different routes to Self-Enhancement for Narcissism and Self-Esteem," *Journal of Research in Personality,* 44(5): 585-592.

Kohut, Heinz (1971). *The Analysis of the Self: A Systematic Approach to the Psychoanalytic Treatment of Narcissistic Personality Disorders.* (International Universities Press, New York).

Krizan, Z., Bushman, B. J. (2011). "Better than my Loved Ones: Social Comparison Tendencies Among

Narcissists," *Personality and Individual Differences,* 50(2): 212-216.

Kubarych, T. S., Deary, I. J., Austin, E. J. (2004). "The Narcissistic Personality Inventory:
Factor Struture in a Non-Clinical Sample," *Personality and Individual Differences,* 36(4): 857-872.

Kubarych, T. S., Deary, I. J., Austin, E. J. (2013). "The Narcissistic Personality Inventory:
Factor Struture in a Non-Clinical Sample," *Personality and Individual Differences,* 45(1): 257-272.

Meier, L. L., Semmer, N. K. (2012). "Lack of Reciprocity and Strain: Narcissism as a Moderator of the Association Between Feeling Under-Benefited and Irritation," *Work & Stress,* 26(1): 56-67.

Morgan, John H. (2015a). *Clinical Psychotherapy: A History of Theory and Practice* (Mishawaka, IN: GTF Books).

Morgan, John H. (2015b). "Palliative Psychotherapy in the Treatment of Geriatric Depression: A Review of Evidence-Based Psychogenic Options," *Innovative Issues and Approaches in Social Sciences,* Vol. 8, No. 1:46-59.

Morgan, John H. (2014a). *Understanding Ourselves: Essays in the History and Philosophy of the Social Sciences* (Mishawaka, IN: GTF Books).

Morgan, John H. (2014b). "The Interpersonal Psychotherapy of Harry Stack Sullivan: Remembering the Legacy," *Journal of Psychology and Psychotherapy,* Volume 4, Issue 6.

Morgan, John H. (2013). "Late-Life Depression and the Counseling Agenda: Exploring Geriatric Logotherapy as a Treatment Modality," *International Journal of Psychological Research*, Vol. VI, #1.

Morgan, John H. (2012a). "Geriatric Logotherapy: Exploring the Psychotherapeutics of Memory in Treating the Elderly," *Psychological Thought, Vol. 5, #2*, 99-105.

Morgan, John H. (2012b). "Pastoral Nurture of the Elderly: The 'Happy Memory' in Geriatric Logotherapy" in *Clinical Pastoral Psychotherapy: A Practitioner's Handbook for Ministry Professionals* Expanded 2nd Edition (Mishawaka, IN: GTF Books).

Morgan, John H. (2012c). "Medication and Counseling in Psychiatric Practice: Biogenic Psychopharmacology and Psychogenic Psychotherapy (Partnering in the Treatment of Mental Illness)," in *Clinical Pastoral Psychotherapy: A Practitioner's Handbook for Ministry Professionals* (Expanded 2nd Edition, Mishawaka, IN: GTF Books).

Morgan, John H. (2012d). *"A Tribute to Carl Rogers," in Clinical Pastoral Psychotherapy: A Practitioner's Handbook for Ministry Professionals* Expanded 2nd Edition (Mishawaka, IN: GTF Books).

Morgan, John H. (2010). *Beginning with Freud: The Classical Schools of Psychotherapy* (Lima, OH: Wyndham Hall Press).

Roche, M. J., Pincus, A. L., Lukowitsky, M. R., Menard, K. S., Conroy, D. E. (2013). "An Integrative Approach to the Assessment of Narcissism," *Journal of Personality Assessment,* 95(3): 237-48.

Stucke, T. S., Sporer, S. L. (2002). "When A grandiose Self-Image is Threatened: Narcissism and Self-Concept Clarity as Predictors of Negative Emotions and Aggression Following Ego-Threat," *Journal of Personality,* 70(4): 509-532.

Tritt, S. M., Ryder, A. G., Ring, A. J., Pincus, A. L. (2010). "Pathological Narcissism and the Depressive Temperament," *Journal of Affective Disorders,* 122(3): 280-284.

Twenge, J. M., Campbell, W. K. (2003). "'Isn't it fun to get the respect that we're going to deserve?' Narcissism, social rejection, and aggression," *Personality & Social Psychology Bulletin,* 29(2): 261-272.

Vater, A., Schroder-Abe, M., Ritter, K., Renneberg, B., Schulze, L., Bosson, J., Roepke, S. (2013). "The Narcissistic Personality Inventory: A Useful Tool for Assessing Pathological Narcissism? Evidence from Patients with Narcissistic Personality Disorder," *Journal of Personality Assessment,* 95(3): 301-308.

ABOUT THE AUTHOR

John Henry Morgan, Ph.D.(Hartford), D.Sc.(London), Psy.D. (Foundation House/Oxford) is the Karl Mannheim Professor of the History and Philosophy of the Social Sciences at the Graduate Theological Foundation in Indiana and was, until his retirement, a Senior Fellow in Behavioral Sciences of Foundation House/Oxford (1995-2015). He has taught a doctoral-level seminar and served as a member of the Board of Studies for twenty years in Oxford University's international summer programs division of the Department for Continuing Education. The author of over thirty books, he has held postdoctoral appointments to Harvard, Yale, and Princeton and is a former National Science Foundation Science Faculty Fellow at the University of Notre Dame. In 2010, he was a Visiting Scholar at New York University and in 2015 was appointed Visiting Scholar at Harvard University for the third time in his academic career. In 2016 he launched an internet newsletter for ministry professionals, *Private Practice: A newsletter for parish clergy considering a professional counseling career.* His latest book, *Geriatric Psychotherapy,* constitutes the third volume in a series preceded by *Clinical Pastoral Psychotherapy: A Practitioner's Handbook for Ministry Professionals* (2012) and *Clinical Psychotherapy: A History of Theory and Practice* (2015).

www.ingramcontent.com/pod-product-compliance
Lightning Source LLC
Chambersburg PA
CBHW070843300326
41935CB00039B/1406